NOTHING IS CERTAIN BUT...

DEATH
AND
TAXES

...UNTIL NOW!!

Published by CelebrityPress®, Orlando, FL.

CelebrityPress® is a registered trademark.

Printed in the United States of America.

ISBN: 978-1-7334176-5-5
LCCN: 2020906707

Most CelebrityPress® titles are available at special quantity discounts for bulk purchases for sales promotions, premiums, fundraising, and educational use. Special versions or book excerpts can also be created to fit specific needs.

For more information, please write:
CelebrityPress®
520 N. Orlando Ave, #2
Winter Park, FL 32789
or call 1.877.261.4930

Visit us online at: www.CelebrityPressPublishing.com

NOTHING IS CERTAIN BUT...

DEATH AND TAXES

...UNTIL NOW!!

Art McPherson & Michael Canet, JD, LLM

CelebrityPress®
Winter Park, Florida

CONTENTS

INTRODUCTION

Tax planning matters.

How often have you started a project at home that you thought you could do yourself that you soon realize you were in way over your head? Whether it's because you tried and didn't finish the effort, or you made a beginner's mistake, most of us are familiar with knowing when a specialist is best served for a particular job. Financial services are no exception. From stocks and investments to tax planning, as an individual you should proceed with extreme caution in an area that relates to your financial future.

Whether you are in the early stages of building your nest egg or meeting personal financial goals, many individuals begin by attempting the "do-it-yourself" approach. As income and wealth increases, it frequently becomes apparent that hiring a professional may make sense. A financial advisor is one such professional, a CPA or a tax accountant is another.

As experts in our field, we have observed all kinds of mistakes that people make when preparing for retirement. *Failing to plan for taxes leading into (and through) retirement is one of the biggest mistakes we regularly see.*

It's surprising in an industry such as this that we see so few professionals addressing clients' needs head-on. Tax planning is greatly important to Americans of all income levels. The majority of clients coming into our firm assume their CPA is maximizing tax savings for them. It's true that most CPAs do a good job on filing returns for their clients. They make sure all the 1099s and

W-2s or K-1s are properly filed, and tell their clients how much they need to send to the IRS. However, this strategy isn't tax planning at its most efficient. What these CPAs typically do not do, at least proactively, is give advice on major tax strategies. The result is missing tax strategies that can save literally hundreds of thousands of dollars in current and future taxes.

We found that most clients need a holistic approach to their retirement. Sometimes, this complete snapshot of their financial life can help avoid costly errors and tax inefficiencies. From our perspective, all investment advice and retirement planning should go through a rigorous tax review to address these inefficiencies. Only through this kind of comprehensive approach can you successfully navigate your retirement into a world of tax-free income.

So, how does this actually work?

WHAT IS PROACTIVE TAX PLANNING?

Let's talk through an example:

Let's say a doctor was getting ready to sell his practice. The gain on the sale was substantial: $3,500,000. He had done a great job preparing for retirement and his nest-egg was almost enough to meet his retirement income needs, and certainly, there were the proceeds from selling his practice – including the real estate that would put him over the top of his income needs and goals for retirement. This doctor was very interested in not only leaving a legacy for his children, but also to contribute to several charitable organizations.

He sat down with his CPA, the same CPA whose firm had handled all of the Doctor's business books and tax returns for years. When the CPA ran numbers for the doctor, he calculated the gain, and explained to the doctor that the tax bill would be about $986,000. That's right: The CPA told the doctor to be prepared to pay almost $1,000,000 in taxes.

...A MILLION DOLLARS IN TAXES!

As you might imagine, the doctor balked at the figure.

When we were presented with the opportunity to run our own scenarios, we stepped up to the challenge.

Want to save a MILLION DOLLARS in TAXES?

The doctor sure did, and we wanted to help him. With a little work and a little creativity, we were able to eliminate almost $900,000 of the tax bill.

CHAPTER 1

WHY TAXES MATTER

At the end of the day, it doesn't matter how much you make, it's how much you keep.

That is a pretty powerful statement when you consider that failing to take into account the impact of taxes on your income both now and in the future, could result in losing thirty, forty, or even fifty percent of your income.

If taxes have that much impact, why is it that so little time is actually spent on tax planning? There are a couple of factors that come into play. Notably, the tax codes change almost every year and there are literally thousands and thousands of pages of codes, regulations, rulings, and IRS guidance on how to apply the code.

During the debates over the 2017 Tax Cuts and Jobs Act, it was widely circulated that there were over 70,000 pages of tax code. While that number isn't quite true, it comes close when considering all the information a person would need to know in order to actually provide smart tax-planning advice.

The tax code has nearly tripled in length over the last 30yrs. Americans deserve a simpler, fairer, and flatter code. (waysandmeans.house.gov/taxreform/)

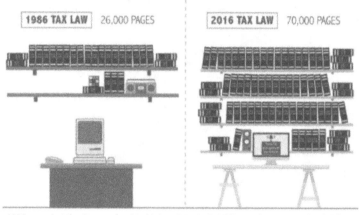

1986 TAX LAW 26,000 PAGES 2016 TAX LAW 70,000 PAGES

With a tax law that has nearly tripled in length in the last 30 years, it is no wonder that 9 out of 10 taxpayers now use either a professional tax preparer or computer software to file their taxes. This blueprint delivers a simpler, fairer, and flatter tax code to help all Americans.

= 1,000 PAGES

Given the limitation of time and expertise, regular Americans feel daunted about what they don't know, and fearful of making errors. Statistically, 9 out of 10 individuals use a professional or computer software for tax filing. Others, of course, prefer to work with individuals who specialize in financial matters. However, even those who have (or hire) a financial advisor face obstacles. For example, most investment firms will not allow their advisors to provide tax guidance. Let that sink in. <u>The person you are relying on to help get you to and through retirement is not allowed to actually help you understand how your investments might be impacted by taxes.</u>

Let's take a look at a very simple example of why taxes matter. Let's assume that you and your spouse have an annual income from work of $100,000. That puts you into the 22% tax bracket. Let's also assume that you take the standard deduction of $24,000. From your investments, your $100,000 mutual fund investment, you receive a 15% capital gain distribution. (Note: this doesn't necessarily mean you actually made money; consider 2008 and 2018, when the overall stock market was negative, many funds reported capitals gains in the 15% range.[1]) Let's also assume you have some savings and received $1,000 in earned interest – at least, here you actually made money.

Here's the math:

W-2 Wages	$100,000
Capital Gains	15,000
Interest	1,000
Total Income	$116,000
Standard Deduction	<24,000>
Taxable Income	$92,000

Tax on $92,000 assuming Federal and 8% State Tax = $20,305. This equates into an effective tax rate of 17.5%.

OK, so what is the point here? If on your $15,000 generated from your investments you are losing 17.5% each year, that tax cost reduces your future nest egg. An 8% return, without this tax bite, over 30 years would grow to almost $151,000. Because of the tax bite, it only grows to just over $102,000. That is almost a 33% reduction in your nest egg...that's each year. That is huge. Would you accept a 33% pay cut? That is what you are doing when you don't pay attention to taxes.

Which brings us back to the point: how can a person provide investment advice without actually understanding the tax implications on that advice? How can you make your own investment decisions if you don't understand the tax implications?

Want further proof that taxes matter? Ask Warren Buffet. He is often quoted as saying that his tax rates are lower than his secretary's. Why is that? Warren has a crack team of tax attorney's at his disposal to take advantage of the tax laws.

---

1. https://www.morningstar.com/articles/890938/more-tax-pain-for-some-mutual-fund-shareholders-in-2018

Buffett does not usually release his tax returns, but he did so in 2010. On his returns, he had an income of $39.8M and paid taxes in the amount of $6.9M. That equates out to about $17.3% effective tax rate. Warren understands that income subject to capital gains rates (currently between ZERO and 15%) is much better than paying taxes at ordinary tax rates (currently up to 40.8%). To clarify: Buffett earned almost $40M and he paid the same tax rate as in our example above of the couple making $116K income. That is why tax planning matters.

Now that we can agree that tax planning matters, let's examine why taxes are poised to increase in the future.

CHAPTER 2

DEBT CLOCKS AND DAVID WALKER

First and foremost, think about the national debt. Is it going up or down?

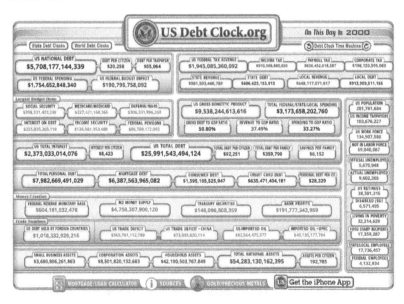

Since 2000, the national debt has gone from just under $6,000,000,000 to almost $26,000,000,000. That is more than a 300% increase in debt.

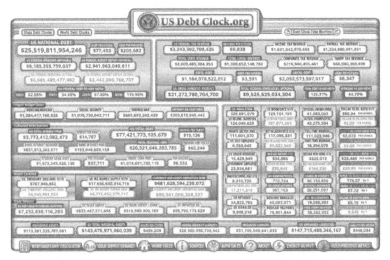

And look at the future obligations from the US DEBT CLOCK.

In 2020, we will need to borrow almost $1T just to pay our bills. That means that almost 20% of our spending is deficit spending: we are borrowing money to pay our bills.[2]

How long can that be sustained without raising taxes at some point in the future? Let's take a look back for some guidance. In 2006, a CPA named David Walker went on a speaking tour and he called it the "Fiscal Wake-Up Tour". During the tour across the country, Walker spoke to local and state governments, politicians, and every group who would take the time to listen to his dire warnings. In 2006, Walker was warning people about a "dirty little secret" everybody in Washington knows – we, as a country, are on a fiscal cliff and if we don't do something to correct it, we will drive right over the edge. In 2006, Walker was warning everybody that the nation's $8.5T debt (now $23.008 trillion as of Oct 31, 2019).

Walker spent almost two years telling anybody and everybody who would listen about how our nation was destined for a dire future if we weren't careful and making changes. He cautioned that now was the time to address these looming issues.

2. https://www.wsj.com/articles/treasury-to-borrow-over-1-trillion-in-2019-for-second-year-in-a-row-11564428624

"Regardless of what politicians tell you, any additional accumulations of debt are... basically deferred tax increases."

Source:
http://www.cnn.com/2009/POLITICS/04/15/walker
.tax.debt/index.html?iref=24hour

Walker wanted to prove and share what he knew in his gut. With just simple math and instruction, Walker explained (to anyone who would listen) how there were not enough revenues coming into the Treasury to pay the bills. As a result, there was not enough money being collected by the U.S. Treasury that was needed to pay the bills of today. Consequently, there was not enough to pay bills that were going to come due in the future. This was a bad scene, and one that would not correct itself without intervention or change.

Back in 2006, his cautions were important, but while he was talking about future obligations in the amount of $40-$50 Trillion dollars, he was actually off by a factor of almost 2 at the time, and this debt has only climbed over time. Presently, we are over $75.5 Trillion in future obligations and the number continues to grow.

Where will that money come from?

Again, Walker openly discussed his ideas, and proved out scenarios using simple math. According to Walker, we would be required to raise taxes AND cut benefits. Here is what he said:

"If Social Security, Medicare, and Medicaid go unchanged, the rate for the lowest tax bracket would increase from 10% to 25%; the tax rate on incomes in the current 25% bracket would have to be increased to 63%, and the tax rate of the highest bracket would have to be raised from 35% to 88%."[3]

3. Source: https://www.cbo.gov/sites/default/files/110th-congress-2007-2008/reports/05-19-longtermbudget_letter-to-ryan.pdf

Who is David Walker, and why does his opinion matter? He was the Comptroller General of the United States during the Clinton and Bush administrations. For those readers who have never heard of this position, the Comptroller General of the United States is the director of the Government Accountability Office, a legislative branch agency established by Congress. It's job? To ensure the fiscal and managerial accountability of the federal government, David Walker was the nation's top accountant and ran the Government Accountability Office, an investigative arm of Congress. He was responsible for making sure the nation's books actually balanced – which for a few short years in the 90's they did. But that stopped dramatically by 2006, which is why Walker spent so much time talking about the dirty little secret.

DEMOGRAPHICS – IT IS ALL ABOUT THE BABY BOOMER

In his now famous interview with CBS' *60 Minutes*, Walker described the problem with baby boomers and their drain on society.

https://www.youtube.com/watch?v=U19_OkPRggE

Walker explains that the baby boomers, considered those born between 1946 and 1964, number about 76 million people. (Immigration offsets deaths so 76 million is still the US Census number.[4]) Starting in 2008, Boomers approaching retirement

---

4. https://www.prb.org/justhowmanybabyboomersarethere/

(age 62 or older) would become eligible for Social Security and by 2011 they would be eligible for Medicare. That isn't the secret.

The secret is that Social Security wasn't designed for 76 million people to collect their benefits for 20 or 30 years. Think back on your economics class from your youth. You may have learned about how Social Security was created, and what it was designed to do. In August of 1935, the life expectancy for the average American was about 58 years of age for men and 62 for women.[5] Even accounting for childhood deaths, only roughly 55% of those who made it to 21 actually lived to collect Social Security.

What does this mean? A significant portion of those who paid into social security either never collected because of early death or had the common courtesy to die shortly after starting to collect their benefits.

On January 31, 1940, the first monthly retirement check was issued to Ida May Fuller of Ludlow, Vermont, in the amount of $22.54. Miss Fuller, a Legal Secretary, retired in November 1939.

Ida May Fuller worked for three years under the Social Security program. The accumulated taxes on her salary during those three years was a total of $24.75. Her initial monthly check was $22.54.

During her lifetime she collected a total of $22,888.92 in Social Security benefits.

This means that on average, most people collected social security for 13-15 years. However, this isn't a futureproof system. There are many variables making this complicated. For example, people are living much longer.[6] A 90-year lifespan is not uncommon; 20% of men and 33% of women who reach age 65 will see their 90th birthday. While that's a lot of happy birthdays, that also means a bigger drain on Social Security and on Medicare resources.[7]

---

5. https://www.ssa.gov/history/lifeexpect.html
6. https://www.ssa.gov/OACT/NOTES/as120/LifeTables_Body.html
7. https://www.hamiltonproject.org/charts/probability_of_a_65_year_old_living_to_a_given_age_by_sex_and_year

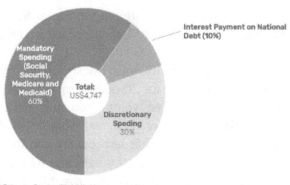

Chart: The Balance · Source: The White House

The U.S. Federal Budget for FY 2020 is $4.7 trillion. That's $2.8 trillion in mandatory spending which includes Social Security, Medicare and Medicaid. That's $1.4 trillion in discretionary spending that includes Defense, Education and Energy. Interest payment on the national debt is $479 billion.

We are currently spending almost 60% of our national revenue on mandatory items, with almost $1.8T just on Social Security and Medicare. And that is with only about halfway through the boomers wanting their benefits – we hit "full" capacity of demand around 2026.

With that as the setting, let's look at the health of the Social Security Trust Fund and how much we have set aside to fund Medicare. According to the 2018 Social Security and Medicare Trust Fund Report, Social Security will be able to pay unreduced benefits until 2034 and Medicare has funding through 2026.[8]

This is an improvement, being fully funded until 2034. As recently as 2010, Social Security was actually posting grim statistics on their annuals statements, warning people that by 2037 recipients would only be receiving about 76 cents on the dollar. That is almost a 25% decrease in income!

For years, the Social Security Administration would send out an annual earnings statement to let you know about your reported earnings and the estimated amount you would receive in Social Security benefits in the future. They also let you know that Social

8. https://www.ssa.gov/oact/TRSUM/

Security was in deep financial trouble, going so far as to include the following paragraphs:

Now, however, the Social Security system is facing serious financial problems, and action is needed soon to make sure the system will be sound when today's younger workers are ready for retirement.[9]

In 2016 we will begin paying more in benefits than we collect in taxes. Without changes, by 2037 the Social Security Trust Fund will be exhausted and there will be enough money to pay only about 76 cents for each dollar of scheduled benefits.[10]

We need to resolve these issues soon to make sure Social Security continues to provide a foundation of protection for future generations.[9]

The shortages faced by Social Security and Medicare go beyond people living longer and the baby boomers wanting their share. Remember that when Social Security first began in 1940, there were 159 workers supporting each recipient. Obviously, in 1940 there were not all that many people actually receiving Social Security benefits. By 1960, there were 5.1 workers for each claimant, and by 2010, there were only 2.9 workers supporting a claimant.[11] That number will continue to drop and by 2035, it is estimated that the number will be closer to 2 to 1.[12]

Our unfunded liabilities, the money we owe for things like Social Security, Medicare, and the Federal Debt, exceeds $122,000,000,000,000. You read that correctly – ONE HUNDRED TWENTY-TWO TRILLION DOLLARS. Where is that money going to come from? Taxes.

Where could tax rates go? No one knows for sure, but certainly we have seen higher tax rates in our lifetimes. Let's reflect back on history of a certain Actor-President for a real-world example. During the 1940's Ronald Reagan was an Actor. As the "story" goes, he was paid about $100,000 per film he made. The problem was, in the 1940's the highest tax rate went all the way up to

---

9. Form SSA-7005-OL (01/15)
10. https://www.ssa.gov/policy/docs/ssb/v70n3/v70n3p111.html
11. https://www.ssa.gov/history/ratios.html
12. https://www.crfb.org/blogs/number-workers-social-security-retiree-declining

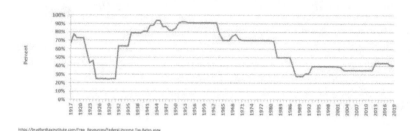

https://bradfordtaxinstitute.com/Free_Resources/Federal-Income-Tax-Rates.aspx

94% on incomes above $200,000. This means that Ronnie would make two movies a year and then pack up his things and go hang out on the ranch with his wife, Jane Wyman. Why? Because he didn't want to work for 6 cents out of every dollar.

By the time he became President in 1981, the top tax rates were 69.13%. That was almost a 25% reduction in tax rates. As we sit here in 2019, tax rates are still 37%. Could they go up? We know they revert back to the former tax rates before the Tax Cut and Jobs Act. That means that people who are currently in the 12-22% tax bracket can expect to be in the 15-25% bracket. And that is if they only just revert back.

Consider the following chart of the 2019 tax brackets:

Tax Bracket / Filing Status	Single	Married Filing Jointly or Qualifying Widow	Married Filing Separately	Head of Household
10%	$0 to $9,700	$0 to $19,400	$0 to $9,700	$0 to $13,850
12%	$9,701 to $39,475	$19,401 to $78,950	$9,701 to $39,475	$13,851 to $52,850
22%	$39,476 to $84,200	$78,951 to $168,400	$39,476 to $84,200	$52,851 to $84,200
24%	$84,201 to $160,725	$168,401 to $321,450	$84,201 to $160,725	$84,201 to $160,700
32%	$160,726 to $204,100	$321,451 to $408,200	$160,726 to $204,100	$160,701 to $204,100
35%	$204,101 to $510,300	$408,201 to $612,350	$204,101 to $306,175	$204,101 to $510,300
37%	$510,301 or more	$612,351 or more	$306,176 or more	$510,301 or more

This income level goes back to 25%-28% tax rates in 2026

Taxes could even go as high as 100%. It doesn't seem possible or realistic, but Ed Slott, the CPA and Retirement Guru tells a story that goes like this. It was around 1975 when John's father died leaving John $1M held inside his father's IRA. It was the only asset his father owned. At the time, the estate tax rules allowed the first $60,000 to be passed tax free, and thereafter, the tax rate was 58%. Because this was the only asset that John received, John had to take the money out of the IRA to pay the estate tax, which resulted in a tax rate of 70% on the withdrawal. Because John lived in California, the State imposed a tax of 11.5%.

Here is the math:

```
$1,000,000  - Inherited from John's Father
   (60,000) - Estate tax exclusion
$  940,000  - Amt. subject to estate tax
  (545,200) - Estate tax that John had to pay from withdrawals
               from the IRA itself
  (381,640) - Federal income tax on the $545,200 John was
               required to pay for estate tax
   (62,698) - California income tax on the $545,200 John had
               to withdraw
$    10,462 - This was the balance left over for John.
```

So, not quite 100% tax, but if you were told you just received a $1,000,000 and after taxes all you had was $10,462, it might feel very much like they took 100% in taxes.

Can taxes go up? This 100% tax rate was available to each and every one of us in 1975. Could it be available again in 2020 or in the future? Time will tell, but given the fact that we as a nation spend more and more money each year and the national debt is growing by Trillions each year, given the fact the future obligations of this country are in excess of $100 Trillion Dollars, and our political leaders seem unable or unwilling to address these spending habits, it would seem that David Walker is correct. These leaders will be forced to raise taxes AND cut benefits.

Ed Slott and David Walker both agree: It does boil down to simple math. The best math results in being in the ZERO income tax bracket. Why ZERO? Being in the ZERO income tax bracket means that if the Federal Government raises taxes by 50%, your tax rate increase is still ZERO. If your State raises taxes by 25%, you are still in the ZERO percent tax bracket. ZERO times any number is still ZERO.

Where to Start:

You would think the starting point is to sit down with your CPA or your investment advisor and create a plan to become more tax efficient. That makes perfect sense and it works in a perfect world. Unfortunately, for many people, their CPA is just somebody who puts numbers on page, and their investment advisor just makes investment recommendations without truly understanding the tax implications.

Bill and Jean came into the office with a very large investment portfolio. They had been working with the same investment firm for years. They had a CPA that had helped them with their very successful business and real estate holdings. They had recently retired and decided to simplify their lives. They sold their business and their real estate and settled into retirement.

When they first came into the office, like any good planning firm should do, we asked to see their tax returns. A tax return really does tell the financial story. We can see pretty much your whole life from your tax return. One of the things we noticed was that they were paying an exorbitant amount of capital gains taxes – to the tune of almost $65,000 a year – just the tax on the capital gains they received each year.

Form 1040 (2018) BIll & Jean SMITH 123-45-6787 Page 2

Attach Form(s) W-2. Also attach Forms(s) W-2G and 1099-R if tax was withheld.	1 Wages, salaries, tips, etc. Attach Form(s) W-2	1		
	2a Tax-exempt interest	2a	b Taxable interest	2b 1,000
	3a Qualified dividends	3a	b Ordinary dividends	3b
	4a IRAs, pensions, and annuities	4a	b Taxable amount	4b
	5a Social security benefits	5a 40,000	b Taxable amount	5b 34,000
	6 Total income. Add lines 1 through 5. Add any amount from Schedule 1, line 22		475,000	6 510,000
Standard Deduction for—	7 Adjusted gross income. If you have no adjustments to income, enter the amount from line 6; otherwise, subtract Schedule 1, line 36, from line 6			7 510,000
• Single or married filing separately, $12,000	8 Standard deduction or itemized deductions (from Schedule A)			8 26,600
• Married filing jointly or Qualifying widow(er), $24,000	9 Qualified business income deduction (see instructions)			9 0
• Head of household, $18,000	10 Taxable income. Subtract lines 8 and 9 from line 7. If zero or less, enter -0-			10 483,400
• If you checked any box under Standard deduction, see instructions.	11 a Tax (see inst) 64,780 (check if any from: 1 ☐ Form(s) 8814 2 ☐ Form 4972 3 ☐)			11 64,780
	b Add any amount from Schedule 2 and check here			
	12 a Child tax credit/credit for other dependents ___ b Add any amount from Schedule 3 and check here			12
	13 Subtract line 12 from line 11. If zero or less, enter -0-			13 64,780
	14 Other taxes. Attach Schedule 4			14 9,880
	15 Total tax. Add lines 13 and 14			15 74,660
	16 Federal income tax withheld from Forms W-2 and 1099			16
	17 Refundable credits: a EIC (see inst.) ___ b Sch 8812 ___ c Form 8863 ___			
	Add any amount from Schedule 5			17
	18 Add lines 16 and 17. These are your total payments			18
Refund	19 If line 18 is more than line 15, subtract line 15 from line 18. This is the amount you overpaid			19
Direct deposit? See instructions.	20a Amount of line 19 you want refunded to you. If Form 8888 is attached, check here			20a
▶ b	Routing number ___ ▶ c Type: ☐ Checking ☐ Savings			
▶ d	Account number ___			
	21 Amount of line 19 you want applied to your 2019 estimated tax ▶ 21			
Amount You Owe	22 Amount you owe. Subtract line 18 from line 15. For details on how to pay, see instructions ▶			22 77,081

> Line 6 includes $25,000 rental income plus $450,000 in capital gain distributions from their mutual fund portfolio. The tax on those capital gains is almost $65,000 as shown on Line 11.

It begged the question, why? When we reviewed the tax return, the first thing we wanted to know was, were they using the income generated by the capital gains, or was it being reinvested into the holdings. Their answer? Reinvestment. Their income needs were being met by their social security, rental income on a building they still did own, and required minimum distributions from their IRA's.

They mentioned that their CPA explained that it was just part of making money. If you make money, you pay taxes. From their CPA's position, that was the nature of investments. Their advisor explained that yes, they paid tax on the money but that means they were making money. The fact is, they were doing pretty well with their investments. The problem was that they were losing so much to tax, and each year they had to take away from their income rather than spend their income; they had to reserve a large portion of that income just to pay the tax on earnings they didn't use. Some taxes? Almost 50% of their monthly income from Social Security, rent(s), and RMD's had to be set aside just to cover the taxes on the investments. Imagine how that impacted their day-to-day living?

They fell into the same trap most people fall into. They relied on trusted advisors to help them with their money, and those advisors didn't truly understand taxes and tax planning.

CHAPTER 3

TAX STRATEGIES THAT WORK

Mutual funds are a very significant portion of many retirees' nest egg. For years, the industry has pushed (think about all the ads you see on TV from mutual fund companies) for people to invest in the stock market via mutual funds. Almost all 401(k)'s are stocked with mutual funds. Even the big wire houses/brokerage firms push mutual funds on their clients (next time your advisor from a big box wire house recommends a mutual fund – ask him/her about soft dollar arrangements...that is for another time). With so much effort out there directing us into mutual funds, is it any wonder that our CPA's and investment advisors don't focus on the tax implications of the very product being pushed?

For Bill and Jean, the solution was quite simple. We suggested an alternative to mutual funds. We provided them two approaches to their tax problems. First, they could transition their portfolio from the tax-heavy mutual funds into the more tax-efficient exchange-traded funds (ETF's).[13] By using exchange-traded funds (ETF's), the capital gains are frequently reduced substantially just by the very nature of how they are structured. While this isn't meant to be a lesson in fund structure, it is important to understand that passive management typically results in less trading within the

---

13. https://www.investopedia.com/articles/investing/090215/comparing-etfs-vs-mutual-funds-tax-efficiency.asp

fund (less trading equates to less capital gains). In addition to reduced internal trading, an ETF trades like an individual stock. This means that you experience capital gains when YOU sell a position, not when other people are redeeming their interest in the mutual fund you also own.

The second option presented was the use of a low-cost, no-load (no commission) annuity. Annuities come with their own particular rules, but by using a no-load annuity, they could maintain their liquidity and by using a low-cost annuity, we didn't run up against the "I-hate-annuities-and-you-should-too" issues; variable annuities are typically deemed to be high expense ratio investment vehicles. What an annuity does do very effectively is eliminate the tax on any capital gains or earnings until such time as you actually use the money.

An Annuity acts like an IRA from the perspective that the investment returns, growth, interest, and capital gains are not taxed until they are actually withdrawn. At such time, any gains are taxed at ordinary tax rates, not capital gain rates.

For Bill and Jean they decided the best option for them was to transition into exchanged-traded funds. By doing so, we were able to eliminate the majority of their capital gain exposure, reducing them down to about $40,000 a year and reduce their taxes substantially: over $70,000 in tax savings just by understanding the tax implications of their investments.

Form 1040 (2018)		Bill & Jean SMITH					123-45-6787		Page 2
Attach Form(s) W-2. Also attach Form(s) W-2G and 1099-R if tax was withheld.	1	Wages, salaries, tips, etc. Attach Form(s) W-2					1		
	2a	Tax-exempt interest	2a		b	Taxable interest	2b	1,000	
	3a	Qualified dividends	3a		b	Ordinary dividends	3b		
	4a	IRAs, pensions, and annuities	4a		b	Taxable amount	4b		
	5a	Social security benefits	5a	40,000	b	Taxable amount	5b	34,000	
	6	Total income. Add lines 1 through 5. Add any amount from Schedule 1, line 22			65,000		6	100,000	
Standard Deduction for—	7	Adjusted gross income. If you have no adjustments to income, enter the amount from line 6; otherwise, subtract Schedule 1, line 36, from line 6					7	100,000	
• Single or married filing separately, $12,000	8	Standard deduction or itemized deductions (from Schedule A)					8	26,600	
• Married filing jointly or Qualifying widow(er), $24,000	9	Qualified business income deduction (see instructions)					9	0	
• Head of household, $18,000	10	Taxable income. Subtract lines 8 and 9 from line 7. If zero or less, enter -0-					10	73,400	
• If you checked any box under Standard deduction, see instructions.	11	a Tax (see inst.) 3,630 (check if any from: 1 ☐ Form(s) 8814 2 ☐ Form 4972 3 ☐)							
		b Add any amount from Schedule 2 and check here ▶ ☐					11	3,630	
	12	a Child tax credit/credit for other dependents b Add any amount from Schedule 3 and check here ▶ ☐					12		
	13	Subtract line 12 from line 11. If zero or less, enter -0-					13	3,630	
	14	Other taxes. Attach Schedule 4					14		
	15	Total tax. Add lines 13 and 14					15	3,630	
	16	Federal income tax withheld from Forms W-2 and 1099					16		
	17	Refundable credits: a EIC (see inst.) b Sch 8812 c Form 8863							
		Add any amount from Schedule 5					17		
	18	Add lines 16 and 17. These are your total payments					18		
Refund	19	If line 18 is more than line 15, subtract line 15 from line 18. This is the amount you overpaid					19		
Direct deposit? See instructions.	20a	Amount of line 19 you want refunded to you. If Form 8888 is attached, check here ▶ ☐					20a		
	b	Routing number ▶ c Type: ☐ Checking ☐ Savings							
	d	Account number							
	21	Amount of line 19 you want applied to your 2019 estimated tax ▶ 21							
Amount You Owe	22	Amount you owe. Subtract line 18 from line 15. For details on how to pay, see instructions ▶					22	3,748	

> As shown in form on page 27, Line 6 still includes $25,000 rental income plus $40,000 in capital gain distributions from their ETF portfolio. The tax on those capital gains is only $3,630 as shown on line 11 *here*. Proper tax planning reduced their taxes by $73,000.

The $70,000 they saved can now be used to further enjoy their retirement, and for Bill and Jean, that meant making annual gifts to their three children. They were able to redirect $70,000 in what would otherwise have gone to the IRS, and instead, gave $20,000 to each of their three kids.

It all starts with understanding taxes.

CHAPTER 4

THE THREE BUCKETS: TAXABLE, TAX-DEFERRED & TAX FREE

You have probably heard the phrase "buckets of money" if you have ever attended a financial workshop or read a book about retirement and money. There are basically three buckets of money out there:

1. **Taxable**
2. **Tax-Deferred**
3. **Tax Free**

As a first step, set up your **Three Buckets** for money and label them accordingly.

There is a mathematically ideal amount of money that should be in each by the time you reach retirement. If you stopped reading here and had to guess, where would you think you'd want the bulk of your money?

How much is the ideal amount to be in each? That is where you need to sit down with a tax planning professional. This isn't necessarily a CPA or Financial Advisor. This is somebody who truly understands tax planning and strategies you can implement today and in the future, with the goal of creating a tax-free retirement and a tax-free legacy for your heirs. The key is that you need to start planning for your tax-free retirement as soon as you possibly can.

Believe it or not, achieving a tax-free retirement is possible for everybody. It doesn't matter if you start the planning early in your working years or if you are already retired. With proper planning and implementing some of the strategies you will find in this book, you may be able to achieve the coveted ZERO percent tax bracket.

BUCKET #1 – THE TAXABLE BUCKET

Let's start with a simple understanding of what each bucket looks like. First, the taxable bucket. This is the bucket that contains assets from which you pay taxes on each year. These are assets and investments like bank accounts, mutual fund accounts, stock accounts, and brokerage accounts.

At the end of every year, the bank issues you a 1099 for the amount of interest you have earned on your accounts. You then report that income on your tax return and pay the taxes accordingly.

Your mutual funds and your brokerage accounts may have a little twist attached to them: capital gains. This is that little stealth "income" you are forced to pay tax on regardless if you sold your mutual fund holdings and regardless if you actually made money on your investment. This is where the difference with working with a tax planner instead of just a financial advisor comes into play.

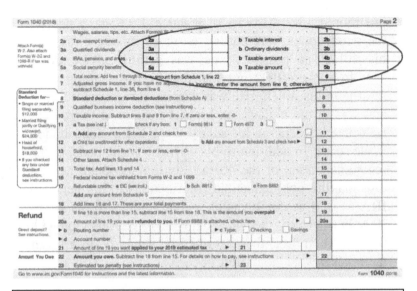

> Your taxable bucket money usually is reported on lines 2 & 3 of your tax return as well as line 6

The problem is you are paying taxes on money you may not need or use. Going back to our simple math from earlier, does it make sense to give up thirty percent or more of your earnings to taxes, especially on money you don't use? To add insult to the tax injury, interest rates are so low at this point, it almost doesn't pay to save in interest-bearing accounts.

BUCKET #2 – THE TAX-DEFERRED BUCKET

If you are receiving a W2 from your employer or even if you are self-employed, you need to sit down and do some math. Remember, it always boils down to simple math: today's tax bracket versus the tax bracket you will be in when you retire. Many of those saving towards retirement and their advisors subscribe to the belief that your retirement income will be in a lower tax bracket when you retire. The thought is that you will need less money during retirement. Why would you want to have less income when you retire?

Greg Jones was an emergency room physician and had

just retired after 40 years of practice. Like many people, the good doctor was putting as much money away into his 401(k) as possible: he was getting advice every year from the 401(k) provider and he was making good returns in his 401(k). He was earning a significant salary and was in the highest tax bracket for almost every year he worked. Reducing his salary via a 401(k) contribution made sense. In addition to his 401(k) contributions, at the recommendation of the 401(k) advisor/custodian, he was also making non-deductible contributions to his personal IRA as well as non-deductible contributions to his wife's IRA. Furthermore, he had actually had a conversation with the 401(k) advisor; they assumed he would be in a lesser tax bracket when he retired.

Why? Why would you be in a lesser tax bracket? Why would you want to be in a lesser tax bracket? It seems that the only reason you might need less money during retirement than during your working years is if you were going to have paid off a mortgage just as you enter into retirement. Even if that is your particular case, it is certain that the "honey-do" list; the "get-around-to-it" list; and the "bucket" list are going to require additional income.

For many retirees, they no longer have the tax deductions they once had. Consider the fact that your mortgage is probably declining which means less mortgage interest deductions.

Many retirees slow down their financial contributions to charity and start volunteering their time. Even those miscellaneous unreimbursed business expenses will be gone. If you or your advisor is suggesting that you will need less income during retirement, you may wish to revisit your math or find a better advisor.

For W2 employees: Tax Strategy #1
The common myth spread by CPA's and financial advisors is that it is better to defer your taxes until the future. The myth is based upon the idea that you will need less money in the future.

This myth has already been debunked: you will probably need as much if not more during retirement, certainly the first five to ten years, as you are actively pursuing those bucket lists.

Here is the old way of thinking: put as much into your 401(k) as your employer will allow, certainly up to any matching they may provide. Hopefully, the goal is to maximize your 401(k) contributions each year. Here is the math:

$50,000	Taxable wages
<10,000>	401(k) contribution which reduces your taxable wages
$40,000	Adjusted taxable wages reported on your tax return

The idea here is that your taxable wages are reduced each year, thereby saving you current tax dollars. The problem is that if you agree that tax rates are going to increase in the future, or even if you think tax rates may stay the same, then you are saving taxes on an apple seed today and being forced to pay taxes on all the apples in the future.

The math suggests that it is better to pay taxes today on the seeds rather than on all the apples that come off the tree:

- Paying tax on the apples: $10,000 deferred today, for 30 years, assuming 6% returns = $57,435. Take that lump sum out, assuming a 25% tax bracket and you have $43,076 in your pocket.

- Paying tax on the seeds: Same $10,000 deferred into a ROTH 401(k) but no tax savings, so the after-tax contribution value (to keep things fair) would be $7,500 (assuming the same 25% tax bracket). Defer for 30 years and assume the same 6% rate of return = $43,076.

Wait, those are the same numbers. Isn't putting money into a ROTH better? Wouldn't it save me taxes in the future? Well, the answer is yes, but... there are many factors and we'll address those a little later in this book. For now, if you choose to put money into a ROTH 401(k) instead of the traditional 401(k) and taxes remain the same, then you are in the exact same position you would have otherwise been in: no harm – no foul.

However if taxes go up even 1%, then paying tax on those seeds today make a difference. If taxes go up as much as David Walker and the Congressional Budget Office have suggested they will, then your decision to pay taxes on the seeds has a profound impact.

Using the same figures but assuming taxes go up just 1%:

- Paying tax on the apples: $10,000 deferred today, for 30 years, assuming 6% returns = $57,435. Take that lump sum out, assuming a 26% tax bracket and you have $42,502 in your pocket.

  This is not a *significant* difference:

  $43,076
  Less: 42,502
  $ 574

What happens if the tax rates go to the 63% bracket as has been suggested? The difference is profound:

- Paying tax on the apples: $10,000 deferred today, for 30 years, assuming 6% returns = $57,435. Take that lump sum out, assuming a 63% tax bracket and you have $42,502 in your pocket.

This is certainly not an *insignificant* difference:

$$\begin{array}{rl} & \$43,076 \\ \text{Less:} & \underline{36,184} \\ & \underline{\$\ 6,892} \end{array}$$

Paying tax on the seed could very well be better than paying tax on all those apples, especially if you think tax rates could go up even 1%, let alone double or more.

BUCKET #3 – THE TAX FREE BUCKET

Consider using your company's ROTH 401(k) instead of the traditional 401(k). Here you pay tax on the seeds instead of the apples. There are rules that need to be followed but this is the first step to tax-free retirement income.

There are a few rules to know when using a ROTH 401(k). First, a ROTH 401(k) is not a ROTH IRA. They both have a few rules in common, but the ROTH IRA has some additional rules to be addressed later. The most important thing to understand about making a contribution to your ROTH 401(k) or ROTH IRA is that you do not receive a tax deduction. Unlike a traditional 401(k) contribution, your contributions to your ROTH 401(k) do not reduce your taxable income. That is the tradeoff: *Pay the tax today to save the taxes later.*

You do have contribution limits: if you are under age 50, for the tax year 2020 you are allowed to contribute up to $19,500. If you are over age 50, there is a tax law provision called "catch up" which will allow you to contribute an additional $6,500. This means that for 2020 you can actually put up to $26,000 of your wages into a ROTH 401(k).

There are also a few rules we need to follow when it comes time to make withdrawals from our ROTHs. First and foremost, the principal, that is, the amount you contributed, is never taxed. Second, you must wait at least five years before you can take the earnings out without being subject to tax. And third, you must be over 59½ to avoid the 10% early withdrawal penalty on those earnings.

The first rule can be easily overlooked. Your contribution is never taxed and is not subject to the 10% early withdrawal rule. In other words, you can contribute to a ROTH and take the principal out whenever you want and not be taxed. That makes sense because you have already paid tax on that money. The second part to this rule, that your principal is not taxed even if withdrawn within 5 years and before 59½, is that you get to tell the IRS whether you have withdrawn earnings or principal or both. You control your tax exposure.

Certainly, there are reasons you would still want to put money into your 401(k), if available. For Greg, the retired doctor, there was most certainly a reason to have that 401(k) in place, but not for the reasons you probably think.

Remember Greg had retired, and when he retired he and his 401(k) advisor, who was also the custodian of the 401(k), discussed rolling the 401(k) into his personal IRA. This makes perfect sense. Combining the accounts makes it easier to calculate RMD's when you turn 70½. An IRA has infinitely more investment options than a traditional 401(k). But for Greg and the advisor, it made sense. The advisor handled the 401(k) rollover and it went perfect:

– Direct rollover.
– No tax on the transfer.
– All handled correctly.

Perfect.

Except it wasn't…

Unfortunately for Greg, the advisor didn't understand the tax implications of combining the two accounts. Remember we said that Greg had been making non-deductible contributions for all those years? By combining the two accounts, Greg eliminated the ability to withdraw those contributions. By combining the two accounts, every time Greg took a dollar out, about five cents was a tax-free return of his principal (remember, a non-deductible contribution is never taxable).

And here was Greg's dilemma, he needed about $200,000 for a down payment on his retirement home he was having built in Florida. The 401(k) advisor told him he could take the money out of his IRA but he would be losing 32% of that money to taxes. The recommendation from the advisor was to take out $290,000 so that he could have about $200,000 in his pocket. He even went to his CPA to calculate the taxes and the "five cents on every dollar he got back tax free."

Our solution was to send him back to work for a month. He got a part-time job at a MinuteClinic as a self-employed, on-call doctor. Over the course of the month, he was paid almost $25,000. This was perfect. Exactly what we wanted. We then opened a 401(k) for the good doctor. He contributed about $21,000 to the 401(k) (this was the maximum he could add to his 401(k) because of FICA issues for self-employed people). The

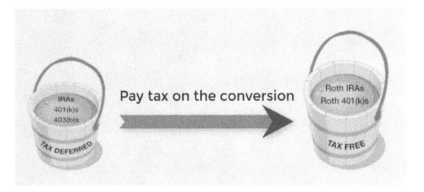

Pay tax on the conversion

goal wasn't to get the $21,000 into a 401(k), the goal wasn't to put the doctor back to work, but the goal was to get a 401(k) open. You see, you can always roll an IRA into a 401(k), and we needed to get the after-tax dollars in that old IRA separated from the pre-tax dollars from the 401(k) rollover. And the beauty of it all is, while you can roll over pre-tax dollars, you can't roll over after-tax contributions.

We "cleaned" the account up. This meant that only after-tax dollars were left in his IRA. Yes, even the earnings on those after-tax dollars could be rolled over, just not the actual after-tax dollars. Once we cleaned up the account, the doctor was able to withdraw the balance from the IRA and use those tax-free funds to purchase his house in Florida.

Tax planning matters ...

CHAPTER 5

FINDING A TAX PLANNER

Tax planning isn't a one-and-done activity. It is something you have to do each and every year. If you are currently working with a professional to prepare your taxes and that person isn't meeting with you several times a year to discuss tax-planning strategies, you are dealing with a tax preparer.

Quite frankly, you can teach a monkey to put numbers on a page. Today's tax software is very powerful and if you answer the questions they ask, you will get a return out of it. The problem here is twofold:

1. Understanding the reason behind the question
2. Answering the question they are asking

You can teach a monkey to put numbers on a page. Doesn't make him more of a tax professional than having a CPA designation.

You may want to use common sense. Tax software doesn't allow for common sense. It has to go through those 70,000 pages or so of tax rules, regulations, codes, and case law to determine what number needs to be put on the page. Ask a question. Get a number.

Working with a CPA does not guarantee you get better results or greater knowledge. Most CPA's are required to only take one tax course in order to qualify to sit for the exam (the requirement is based upon the underlying degree from a College or University; most accounting programs only require one class in taxation to receive a business or accounting degree). Even a CPA who has been preparing taxes for years may not offer tax planning services to their clients.

CPA's do provide services like accounting and payroll. A good example of this is Cliff. Cliff owned a *Snap-On* tool company. You probably have seen their trucks around town. They go from auto shop to auto shop supplying mechanics their tools. As a small business, it provided Cliff and his wife a comfortable living, but it took a lot of work keeping track of mileage, inventory, sales, accounts receivable, and all the other aspects of owning a small business. Cliff actually had a CPA firm doing his books for him and preparing his Schedule C each and every year. They told him how much to send in for estimated taxes. They told him how much profit he had. They even told him how much to put into his IRA every year. They were a good CPA firm. They didn't actually provide planning services, just made sure his numbers were in the right spot. Cliff thought he had found a good tax professional.

Ask The Right Questions

If you want to work with a tax professional or an investment professional who does tax planning, you have to specifically ask if they provide *planning* services or just *preparation* services.

Ask the following questions:

1. How often do we meet to discuss taxes?
2. Did the planner ask you to bring in your tax returns to review?
3. Do they consider more than the current year in their planning?
4. How do they address retirement income?
5. Do they recommend various "money buckets"?
6. How long have they been providing planning services?
7. Will my Social Security be taxable?
8. Can you create a plan to get me to the ZERO percent tax bracket?

These are not simple questions and should not result in yes or no answers. They should respond with questions about where your money is currently held: taxable buckets, tax-free buckets, and tax-deferred buckets. They should ask about your income needs and discuss how long before you retire. They should address a whole list of scenarios and be able to explain how they can attack the tax bite you may face in the future. Before they even give you advice, they always ask to see your investments, make sure they are also asking to see your tax returns. That should be part of the advice they are providing. *It doesn't matter how much you make, it is how much you keep.*

That is what we had in mind for Cliff. Fortunately, he came to us before he finalized his tax return:

…For Cliff, the CPA was a person putting numbers on a page.
…For Cliff, his advisor was just facilitating the IRA contributions.
…<u>For Cliff, he had no tax planning</u>.

The CPA took Cliff's *QuickBooks* and extracted the numbers from the P&L and put them into the return. The CPA told Cliff to make an IRA contribution for himself and his wife. The CPA told Cliff that he would be writing a big check this year, a very large check. Cliff was shocked. He was confused. His income wasn't that much larger than normal. If fact, when he came to see us, the first thing we did was fix this horrible tax issue.

Here was the problem. While Cliff made a comfortable living with his tool company, the cost of health insurance for a small businessman, like for many of us, was sky rocketing. He actually qualified for assistance under the Affordable Care Act. The ACA actually provided him with an upfront stipend to help pay the monthly premium. The ACA also had rules that needed to be followed. One of these rules was a strict adherence to income. If a participant went one dollar over the threshold, they were forced to pay back their entire subsidy. All of it. Plus there could be penalties. Cliff was over the threshold and was in tax trouble. The CPA solution was to pay the tax bill.

In Cliff's case, we recommended opening a 401(k). By using a 401(k), he was able to put more money into the retirement account than he would have been by using a traditional IRA. In fact, we were going to use the same $12,000 he was going to contribute to his and his wife's IRA's, that total went into the 401(k). That didn't really make a difference as far as the ACA and tax bill, after all $12,000 out of left pocket or out of the right pocket is still $12,000 out of the pocket. The CPA was quick to point this out when we suggested to her that Cliff use a 401(k) instead of an IRA. Understanding how taxes work and tax planning, that was the difference we shared with the CPA.

You see, 401(k) rules allow for the company, the company he owned, to share their profits (i.e., his profits) via a profit-sharing contribution to his 401(k). That is correct. In addition to "his" contributions to the 401(k), which reduce his personal income, the company can also make a contribution (called a profit-sharing match). This contribution also reduces Cliff's total taxable income, but more importantly, it reduces his Business Income. Because of the nature of the ACA, reducing Cliff's income by making IRA contributions wasn't enough. We needed to reduce the income of the business as well. This allowed him to qualify for the ACA and therefore he didn't have to repay the subsidy the CPA had him paying. Tax savings: just under $17,500.

Tax Planning Matters ...

Sitting down with your investment advisor probably isn't the solution either. If you have ever looked closely at your statements from your broker, they usually have a little statement along the lines of:

- *For tax advice, please consult with a qualified tax advisor, CPA, or financial planner – Charles Schwab.*

OR

- *Wells Fargo Advisors is a trade name used by Wells Fargo Clearing Services, LLC, a registered broker-dealer and non-bank affiliate of Wells Fargo & Company. We are not a legal or tax advisor.*

OR

- *Merrill Lynch would like you to note the following items(s) which may affect your tax return. Please discuss these matters with your Tax Advisor prior to completing your return.*

... and the list goes on.

Most investment professionals are not trained in and do not understand the complexities of tax planning. They may know simple rules such as Required Minimum Distributions (even then there are disclaimers about talking to a tax professional), the difference between capital gains and ordinary income, and that Social Security may in fact be taxable. They are not tax planners, and most often they make it clear you need to talk to a tax professional. And therein lies the problem.

For many of those contemplating or entering into retirement, this is their first true encounter with a financial planning professional.

Most advisors will gather some information about you and your situation: age, retirement date, assets, Social Security income, pension income, and a few other details like risk tolerance and the names of your heirs. They then compile a plan, based upon your risk tolerance, on how much money they think you can take from the portfolio they recommend to you. They may even take into account the fact that you will pay taxes, but more often than not, they are not making suggestions on how to allocate your investments based upon taxes. They want returns and growth; you want to know how much you actually get to keep.

Susan was this typical soon-to-be retiree. She was recently divorced and was going to receive a portion of her husband's pension, it was a small amount, but every penny counts when you are going from having a paycheck every two weeks to being unemployed for the next thirty years! She was going to collect Social Security. She had a small 401(k) of her own. And she also had a very large equity position in a very specific stock. In fact, it was a stock that had been handed down over the generations. It was stock from the original building of N.Y. City's Empire State Building. It was quite a story to hear about the changes and iterations of the ownership over the decades. Susan loved sharing the story because it was part of her history.

When Susan sat down with her advisor, he explained to her that she would need to sell her investment of stock in order to diversify (sounds reasonable) and once she sold and diversified, she would be able to use those proceeds to help create the income she needed during retirement. The advisor had a simple approach: there was an income need. There was income from pensions and Social Security, there was an RMD calculation that would produce X dollars from her IRA, and finally, to secure her income, he wanted to invest a large portion of the proceeds from the sale of stock into an annuity.

As Susan understood, the annuity would guarantee her an income stream, regardless of the market conditions, for the remainder of her life. Again, all this sounds reasonable (you can argue the pros and cons of using annuities but that is another story).

When Susan presented her plan to her CPA who she had been using for decades, the CPA asked about the basis of the stock so that the CPA could calculate the taxes Susan would have to send to the IRS. Susan explained the history of inheriting the stock from her Grandfather almost 40 years ago. She explained the buying and selling of the company itself over the years (this was a privately held stock for a number of years) and based upon those facts, the CPA calculated that Susan would have a gain of about $400,000 and be paying a tax of about $85,000.

Susan was a bit surprised but understood that with the sale of the stock, per the advice of her financial advisor, would come a tax bill. She understood the need to create income and she understood the need for diversification. It all sounded reasonable.

Then her kids found out what she was doing and asked her to sit down with us and allow us to review the plan the advisor had created. Immediately, our concern was focused on two issues: the basis of the stock being sold, and also on the investment recommendations being made.

Susan explained to us that the CPA had been doing her taxes since she inherited the stocks from her Grandfather. In fact, she had the original transfer paperwork for the inheritance and it actually had a price per share on the document. We had a starting point. We then asked her whether she had been receiving dividends and distributions over the years and the answer was yes. As a matter of fact, the CPA had shown her every year how much she was earning on the inheritance. This meant that we had a record of each financial transaction that happened in the past.

You see, for Susan, each time she received a dividend on paper, the company actually kept the dividends for operating expenses. This meant that all those dividends actually added to her basis. By the time we were done reviewing and analyzing her taxes, we were able to reduce them to just a $37,000 gain. But the good news didn't end there.

We also did some tax planning for her based upon the recommendations of her advisor. Susan had told her advisor that she wanted $80,000 a year to live on. It was a nice retirement. The advisor knew she would receive about $18,000 in pensions and Social Security receipts. That left him to cover the balance of $62,000 per year. In order to do this he recommended using an annuity. The annuity would produce the $62,000 per year she wanted if she put just over $900,000 into the contract. By happenchance, that was about the balance left over after paying her tax bill, according to the return her CPA wanted to file.

Here is the problem we had (and there were several) from a tax perspective. The advisor was solving an income issue but ignoring the tax issue. By using her after tax dollars and putting them into an annuity, he did create the income she wanted but in doing so made the growth, interest, and earnings that came out of the annuity all taxed at ordinary tax rates. The tax bill wasn't pretty AND it actually resulted in her having less than the $80,000 she wanted, remember there was a tax bill due each year.

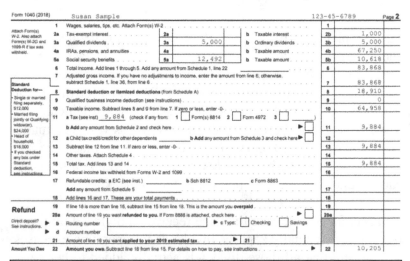

The original plan resulted in an initial tax bill of almost $85,000 and future tax bills in excess of $10,000 with a resulting income of just under $74,000 per year

After reviewing Susan's taxes and investment options with her, we made a few adjustments. We wanted to preserve the capital gains nature of her investments. What the CPA failed to explain, what the investment advisor didn't understand, and what Warren Buffet knows all too well, is when you can't have tax-free income, have capital gains. Why? Because if you handled capital gains correctly, your capital gains rate is ZERO. That means you pay no tax on your capital gains.

) (2018)		Susan Sample							123-45-6789		Page 2
	1	Wages, salaries, tips, etc. Attach Form(s) W-2							1		
(s) tach	2a	Tax-exempt interest	2a			b	Taxable interest		2b	1,000	
IG and x was	3a	Qualified dividends	3a	40,000		b	Ordinary dividends		3b	5,000	
	4a	IRAs, pensions, and annuities	4a			b	Taxable amount		4b	5,250	
	5a	Social security benefits	5a	12,492		b	Taxable amount		5b	10,618	
	6	Total income. Add lines 1 through 5. Add any amount from Schedule 1, line 22			37,000				6	58,868	
	7	Adjusted gross income. If you have no adjustments to income, enter the amount from line 6; otherwise, subtract Schedule 1, line 36, from line 6							7	58,868	
for—	8	**Standard deduction or itemized deductions** (from Schedule A)							8	20,785	
harried ately,	9	Qualified business income deduction (see instructions)							9	0	
ng ualifying	10	Taxable income. Subtract lines 8 and 9 from line 7. If zero or less, enter -0-							10	38,083	
	11	a Tax (see inst) _____ (check if any from: 1 ☐ Form(s) 8814 2 ☐ Form 4972 3 ☐ _____)									
		b **Add** any amount from Schedule 2 and check here						▶	11		
	12	a Child tax credit/credit for other dependents _____ b Add any amount from Schedule 3 and check here ▶ ☐							12		
	13	Subtract line 12 from line 11. If zero or less, enter -0-							13		
ked der	14	Other taxes. Attach Schedule 4							14		
	15	Total tax. Add lines 13 and 14							15		
tions	16	Federal income tax withheld from Forms W-2 and 1099							16		
	17	Refundable credits: a EIC (see inst.) _____ b Sch 8812 _____ c Form 8863 _____									
		Add any amount from Schedule 5 _____							17		
	18	Add lines 16 and 17. These are your total payments							18		
}	19	If line 18 is more than line 15, subtract line 15 from line 18. This is the amount you overpaid							19		
	20a	Amount of line 19 you want **refunded to you.** If Form 8888 is attached, check here						▶ ☐	20a		
it? ions	b	Routing number _____				▶ c Type: ☐ Checking ☐ Savings					
	d	Account number _____									
	21	Amount of line 19 you want **applied to your 2019 estimated tax** ▶ 21									
u Owe	22	**Amount you owe.** Subtract line 18 from line 15. For details on how to pay, see instructions						▶	22		

By preserving the capital gains aspect of Susan's income, she now enjoys just over $95,000 a year of tax-free income.

Susan's income has increased by over 20% and she now pays ZERO taxes.

Tax planning matters ...

UNDERSTANDING TAX FREE

If you didn't know anything else at this point, which bucket would you chose to hold the majority of your money? At the end of the day, there is a mathematically correct amount of money to have in each of the three buckets.

What exactly constitutes tax free? There are three basic vehicles that provide for tax-free income. Before we get there, we need to take a step back and examine social security again.

It is often thought that Roosevelt said, "Social Security would never be taxed." In fact, there were several administrative rulings from the Treasury in the 30's and 40's that exempted Social Security payments from tax. This was true all the way up to 1983. In 1981, President Reagan and Congress passed the Economic Recovery Tax Act and the ensuing taxes changes, including The Equity and Fiscal Responsibility Act of 1982 and the 1983 Amendments to the Social Security Act, resulted in up to 50% of Social Security being exposed to taxes. In 1993, as part of the Omnibus Budget Reconciliation Act, up to 85% of Social Security was now subject to tax exposure.[14]

Here is how this works:

First you add up all your provisional income. Your provisional income is basically all your income which will appear on your tax return except social security. The rule requires you to include all the income that will show up on the return but does not allow you to take any of the adjustments that would reduce your income. For example, you do not reduce your provisional income by your IRA contributions, your self-employment health care deductions, or any of those items that are included in calculating your Modified Adjusted Gross Income.

---

14. https://www.ssa.gov/history/taxationofbenefits.html

7	Wages, salaries, tips, etc. Attach Form(s) W-2	7	
8a	Taxable interest. Attach Schedule B if required	8a	
b	Tax-exempt interest. **Do not** include on line 8a . . . **8b**		
9a	Ordinary dividends. Attach Schedule B if required	9a	
b	Qualified dividends . . . **9b**		
10	Taxable refunds, credits, or offsets of state and local income taxes	10	
11	Alimony received	11	
12	Business income or (loss). Attach Schedule C or C-EZ	12	
13	Capital gain or (loss). Attach Schedule D if required. If not required, check here ▶ ☐	13	
14	Other gains or (losses). Attach Form 4797	14	
15a	IRA distributions **15a** **b** Taxable amount	15b	
16a	Pensions and annuities **16a** **b** Taxable amount	16b	
17	Rental real estate, royalties, partnerships, S corporations, trusts, etc. Attach Schedule E	17	
18	Farm income or (loss). Attach Schedule F	18	
19	Unemployment compensation	19	
20a	Social security benefits **20a** **b** Taxable amount	20b	
21	Other income. List type and amount	21	
22	Combine the amounts in the far right column for lines 7 through 21. This is your **total income** ▶	22	

Provisional income consists of those income items that would normally appear on the "top" of the tax return PLUS amounts found on line 8b: tax free interest.

23	Educator expenses	23	
24	Certain business expenses of reservists, performing artists, and fee-basis government officials. Attach Form 2106 or 2106-EZ	24	
25	Health savings account deduction. Attach Form 8889	25	
26	Moving expenses. Attach Form 3903	26	
27	Deductible part of self-employment tax. Attach Schedule SE	27	
28	Self-employed SEP, SIMPLE, and qualified plans	28	
29	Self-employed health insurance deduction	29	
30	Penalty on early withdrawal of savings	30	
31a	Alimony paid **b** Recipient's SSN ▶	31a	
32	IRA deduction	32	
33	Student loan interest deduction	33	
34	Tuition and fees. Attach Form 8917	34	
35	Domestic production activities deduction. Attach Form 8903	35	
36	Add lines 23 through 35	36	
37	Subtract line 36 from line 22. This is your **adjusted gross income** ▶		

Provisional income does not allow you to reduce your income by the modifications.

Once you have calculated your provisional income (don't forget to include muni-bond and other tax-free interest into the calculation), you add that to one-half of your Social Security.

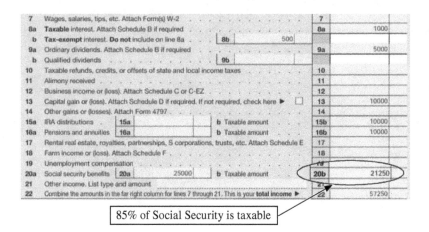

85% of Social Security is taxable

Here the provisional income is calculated as follows:

Taxable Interest	$ 1,000	
Tax Free Interest	500	
Dividends	5,000	
Capital Gains	10,000	
IRA Distribution	10,000	
Pension	10,000	
Subtotal	$36,500	
½ of SS of 25,000	12,500	
Total:	$49,000	

Married Filing Jointly

Provisional Income	% of Social Security Subject to Tax
Under $32,000	0%
$32,000 to $44,000	50%
Over $44,000	85%

Single Filers

Provisional Income	% of Social Security Subject to Tax
Under $25,000	0%
$25,000 to $34,000	50%
Over $34,000	85%

So what counts as tax free? Any item that does not include causing Social Security to be subject to taxation. For our conversation, those three categories are ROTH 401(k)'s, ROTH IRA's, and properly designed cash value life insurance. We have already explained how the ROTH 401(k) works. Let's examine the other two sources of tax-free income.

First, the ROTH IRA. The ROTH IRA shares the same features as a ROTH 401(k). They both have a 5-year requirement to avoid tax on the growth. They both have 59½ to avoid penalties on withdrawals of growth. Where they differ dramatically is in the ability to contribute to them. The ROTH 401(k) has no income limitations on a person's ability to contribute to their ROTH 401(k).

Conversely, the ROTH IRA does have restrictions on the ability to contribute. First, you must have income to contribute. For our purposes, this means either you have wages that are reported on a W-2 or you are self-employed, and your profit is subject to FICA (Social Security and Medicare taxes). If you have income, you are eligible to contribute to your ROTH IRA. In 2020, for people under age 50, you can contribute up to $6,000 (your contribution is subject to your earnings; you cannot contribute more than you make) and if you are over 50, you can contribute a "catch up" of an additional $1,000. So, for 2020, you can contribute up to $7,000 of your wages into a ROTH IRA.

The next rule that needs to be observed is your total income. While there are no earning limitations on the ROTH 401(k), there are limitations when it comes to contributing to a ROTH IRA. For single filers, the 2020 rules begin to limit your allowable contributions when your income reaches $124,000, and by the time your income exceeds $139,000, your ability to contribute is completely phased out. For married filers, the phase out begins at $196,000 and ends at $203,000. Basically, if you make too much money, you can't take advantage of a ROTH IRA.

However, for those constrained by the income limitations, lucky you, there are strategies to work around the rules. This is where tax planning comes into play again. What is the strategy? It is called a "back door ROTH". The idea is similar in nature to what we did for Doctor Jones when he had rolled his 401(k) into his non-deductible IRA.

Here is what you do: make a non-deductible IRA contribution. You can then immediately convert the non-deductible IRA into a ROTH. For conversions, there are no income rules. This means that anybody, regardless of income, can convert from an IRA or 401(k) (or other company sponsored retirement plan) into a ROTH IRA, thereby turning what would otherwise be a taxable account into a lifetime of tax-free income for you and your heirs.

ROTH CONVERSIONS

Pay tax today at lower tax rates to have tax-free money later when tax rates are higher.

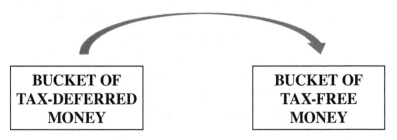

| BUCKET OF TAX-DEFERRED MONEY | BUCKET OF TAX-FREE MONEY |

The idea behind a ROTH Conversion is that we want to move our money from a tax-deferred bucket and pay taxes at today's rates so that when we use the money down the road, the money is tax free. This goes back to the idea of paying tax on the seed instead of the apple. Before you jump aboard the conversion band wagon, it does take a little math and strategy to determine if conversion makes sense for you.

Remember Bill and Jean? Their capital gains problem was just the tip of the iceberg. When we were reviewing their investments and retirement plan, we discovered another inconsistency between good planning, their advisor, and their CPA. Their advisor actually told them to convert some of their IRA money into ROTH. Sounds like good advice, right? They took that advice to their CPA and during the meeting, without any actual review or analysis done, the CPA said converting wasn't a good idea. Bill and Jean had a real problem. One hand was saying convert and the other hand was saying <u>not</u> to convert. The advisor was telling them that they would save taxes later. The CPA was saying the tax consequences today were too drastic.

If you remember, Bill and Jean were real big on helping their kids out. They also had all the income they needed, and because we suggested they restructure their investments, they had more than enough cash flow to meet their needs without actually using the RMD's they were being forced to take out each year.

Comparison of Alternatives

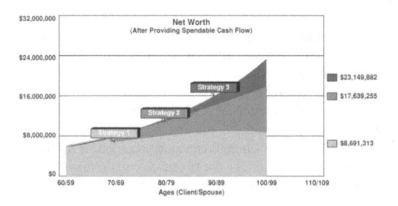

What Bill and Jean wanted to know was if it made sense to convert from their traditional IRA to the ROTH. The answer for them was yes. It made sense, but first they wanted to understand the rules of how and why. Those rules, while they seem simple and straightforward enough, are actually quite complicated.

The first thing that needs to be considered is what tax rate are you in today and what tax rate will you be in when you retire. IF you are already retired, this turns out to be an easy exercise. The tricky part is what will your tax rates be like when you retire. It is a bit like hitting a moving target. Do you just use the existing tax rates and assume what your income needs will be? Obviously you will need to take into account your sources of income: pensions, Social Security, investments, real estate, retirement accounts and wherever else your income might flow. Once you know your income sources, you then have to run tax calculations on those flows.

Once you have calculated those taxes. You then have to run your current income and add in the amount you might want to convert from your retirement accounts to your ROTH account. Remember, you have to pay tax when you move your assets from the traditional IRA/401(k) into the ROTH IRA (this is called a conversion). What tax bracket will you be in if you choose to convert. There is a tax bill due. You are paying the tax today so that in theory, you will save in taxes later.

In addition to determining what the additional tax will be, you also have to determine from where will the tax bill be paid. Paying for the tax bill due out of the conversion itself could be an option. But remember, if you were to use the actual IRA itself to pay the tax bill, it counts as a withdrawal and therefore could be subject to a 10% penalty if you are under age 59½. And, the use of the IRA money itself could mean it takes longer for the ROTH to actually "catch up" for the tax money withdrawn. You might be better off paying for tax from dollars that are already taxed: use the taxable bucket!

Net Worth*			Wealth to Heirs		
Strategy 1	Strategy 2	Strategy 3	Strategy 1	Strategy 2	Strategy 3
47.14%	23.57%	Tax Efficient	47.14%	23.57%	Tax Efficient
6,001,533	6,001,533	5,981,920	5,616,080	5,616,080	7,845,257
6,206,025	6,206,025	6,092,442	5,759,345	5,759,345	7,915,158
6,381,616	6,381,616	6,247,906	5,926,667	5,926,667	8,011,448
6,580,228	6,580,228	6,428,849	6,114,244	6,114,244	8,129,419
6,784,329	6,784,329	6,618,050	6,307,188	6,307,188	8,251,633
6,994,032	6,994,032	6,829,124	6,505,624	6,505,624	8,378,307
7,209,452	7,209,452	7,049,385	6,709,675	6,709,675	8,509,680
7,430,702	7,430,702	7,279,343	6,919,468	6,919,468	8,646,000
7,657,898	7,657,898	7,519,546	7,135,130	7,135,130	8,787,535
6,707,174	7,891,150	7,770,562	7,266,608	7,356,785	8,934,568
6,834,439	8,130,571	8,046,896	7,397,390	7,584,561	9,158,314
6,961,475	8,375,902	8,333,064	7,527,201	7,821,455	9,389,739
7,088,059	8,627,166	8,629,292	7,655,746	8,064,918	9,629,085
7,213,944	8,884,370	8,935,813	7,782,702	8,315,041	9,838,705
7,338,869	9,147,506	9,252,846	7,907,726	8,571,916	10,024,173
7,462,544	9,416,557	9,580,610	8,030,444	8,835,623	10,216,748
7,584,663	9,691,477	9,919,290	8,150,455	9,106,229	10,416,709
7,704,892	9,972,223	10,269,078	8,267,327	9,383,695	10,624,167
7,822,878	10,258,720	10,630,154	8,380,601	9,595,254	10,839,585
7,938,230	10,550,882	11,002,798	8,489,773	9,809,093	11,063,058
8,050,539	10,848,607	11,387,275	8,594,317	10,028,978	11,294,873
8,159,361	11,151,771	11,783,807	8,693,657	10,254,981	11,535,326
8,264,218	11,460,222	12,192,842	8,787,184	10,487,158	11,784,713
8,364,598	11,773,789	12,615,130	8,874,239	10,725,549	12,043,341
8,459,957	12,092,269	13,051,493	8,954,124	10,970,179	12,311,520
8,549,703	12,415,459	13,503,030	9,026,083	11,220,729	12,589,212
8,633,210	12,743,135	13,971,591	9,089,319	11,477,061	12,850,281
8,709,806	13,075,049	14,458,807	9,142,971	11,739,079	13,082,851
8,778,772	13,410,927	14,967,649	9,186,126	12,006,646	13,322,482
8,839,339	13,750,466	15,502,072	9,217,803	12,279,580	13,606,483
8,890,688	14,093,381	16,062,248	9,236,962	12,557,177	13,959,036
8,931,940	14,439,371	16,644,823	9,242,488	12,838,992	14,311,114
8,962,163	14,788,117	17,251,244	9,233,198	13,064,277	14,676,916
8,980,358	15,139,289	17,883,309	9,207,827	13,309,355	15,057,314
8,985,460	15,492,578	18,543,373	9,165,025	13,536,491	15,453,176
8,976,336	15,847,692	19,233,623	9,103,360	13,765,391	15,865,476
8,951,776	16,204,325	19,952,528	9,031,369	13,995,803	16,314,839

For Bill and Jean, using their taxable account to pay the tax bill meant that the breakeven point was 13 years. This means that paying tax on the seeds took 13 years to make sense. From that point forward, it was beneficial for them from a net worth point of view. Net worth does not equate to income. Net worth, in this example, just means that if Bill and Jean were to take all their money out of all their accounts, paying any tax due at the time, their net worth would be $8,627,166 IF they did NOT convert. By converting, their net worth would be $8,629,292. Not a lot at that point of time, but it is just one measurement of whether it makes sense to convert or not.

For Jean and Bill, the conversion made sense from the perspective of more net worth for them while they were alive, but also more after-tax value going to their children upon their death. But that was not the deciding factor. The real reason it made sense to them was that it eliminated their income yearly income tax bill. We could get them to the point of ZERO percent tax rates.

CHAPTER 6

UNDERSTANDING REQUIRED MINIMUM DISTRIBUTIONS (RMD)

Bill and Jean are not unlike many retirees who have been good stewards of their money. They have made smart choices and saved over their lifetime in order to be in a position to enjoy the retirement they envisioned. For many people, until the day actually arrives, it is hard to picture what retirement really looks like. When Bill and Jean sat down with the advisor, he went through their income and explained how he was going to create the income they needed during their retirement. During that conversation, he explained to Bill and Jean that once they turned 70½, the IRS was going to require them to take money out of their retirement accounts, even if they didn't need the income.

Let's take a minute and ponder what that looks like in real terms:

⇨ You are being forced to take withdrawals from your retirement savings even if you don't want or need the money.
⇨ You have made all the sacrifices to save the money.
⇨ You have paid all the fees (hidden or otherwise).
⇨ And you have taken all the risk associated with the investments.

Yes, you did get a tax break for saving in your retirement accounts, and because of that, the IRS now wants their share of your hard-earned money.

To add insult to injury, in the news there are reports of different groups scamming and taking advantage of retirees: identity theft, pending lawsuit claims, Social Security impersonation, romance scams, calls from "grandchildren-in-trouble" scams, computer support scams, winning the lottery scams, IRS collection scams, and the list goes on. The one that nobody actually mentions? … The RMD scam.

Did you know that if you fail to file a return your tax penalty is up to 25%? That is right, if you just don't file your returns each year, your penalty is up to 25%. Filing your taxes but not paying? That penalty is only ½ percent per month. What is the penalty for not taking enough money out of your retirement accounts each year? FIFTY PERCENT! That is right, not making the correct RMD calculation and withdrawing it correctly is a 50% penalty, PLUS, you still have to pay the tax. Imagine that scenario:

RMD amount	$2,000
Penalty (50%)	$1,000
Tax (22%)	$ 440

Out of your $2,000 required minimum distribution of $2,000, you lose 72% to taxes. To make matters worse, the IRS doesn't make the RMD calculation easy. Every year the numbers change. To calculate your RMD, you must first start with the 12/31 balance of your retirement accounts from the prior year. In 2020 you will calculate the amount you must withdraw based upon the 12/31/2019 account values. That seems easy enough.

The next step is a little trickier. You must then go to the IRS lifetime tables… *tables, plural!* There is one table for you. There is another table if you are married and your spouse is ten years younger than you. There is yet another table for non-spouse beneficiaries that in itself has three different options and calculations. The IRS couldn't just make it simple and require you take a simple percentage every year. Nope. They change the percentage each year.

To further complicate the rules, you must take RMD's from each category of retirement account you own: IRA, 401(k), 403(b), 457, profit sharing, etc. But wait, it gets even more complicated. Let's say you have IRA's at three banks and two 401(k)'s – one from your employer from whom you just retired and one from an old job. You must calculate your RMD's for each of the accounts individually. You can then take the RMD requirement from a single account. As long as the single account is like the other accounts. Huh?

Your investment company may issue you an IRS form 5498 or otherwise calculate your RMD's on your behalf. Please note that the 5498 does come with a disclosure about consulting with a tax advisor to make sure your calculations are done correctly.

For example, let's assume you have the following three IRA's:

Bank #1	$ 20,000
Bank #2	30,000
Bank #3	<u>50,000</u>
Total IRA Values 12/31	<u>$100,000</u>

In addition, let's also assume the following 401(k)'s:

Job #1	$300,000
Job #2	<u>$100,000</u>
Total 401(k) values 12/31	<u>$400,000</u>

Uniform Lifetime Table

Age	Life Expectancy Factor	Age	Life Expectancy Factor
70	27.4	82	17.1
71	26.5	83	16.3
72	25.6	84	15.5
73	24.7	85	14.8
74	23.8	86	14.1
75	22.9	87	13.4
76	22.0	88	12.7
77	21.2	89	12.0
78	20.3	90	11.4
79	19.5	91	10.8
80	18.7	92	10.2
81	17.9	93	9.6

The older you get, the greater the percentage you are required to take out of your retirement accounts. At age 70, the RMD is just over 3.6%. By the time you reach age 90 that percentage is just under 9%. If you happen to make it to age 100, you are being forced to withdraw almost 16% per year.

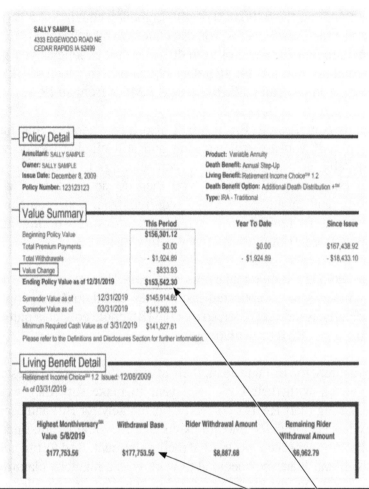

SALLY SAMPLE
4333 EDGEWOOD ROAD NE
CEDAR RAPIDS IA 52499

Policy Detail

Annuitant: SALLY SAMPLE
Owner: SALLY SAMPLE
Issue Date: December 8, 2009
Policy Number: 123123123

Product: Variable Annuity
Death Benefit: Annual Step-Up
Living Benefit: Retirement Income Choice℠ 1.2
Death Benefit Option: Additional Death Distribution +℠
Type: IRA - Traditional

Value Summary

	This Period	Year To Date	Since Issue
Beginning Policy Value	$156,301.12		
Total Premium Payments	$0.00	$0.00	$167,438.92
Total Withdrawals	- $1,924.89	- $1,924.89	- $18,433.10
Value Change	- $833.93		
Ending Policy Value as of 12/31/2019	$153,542.30		

Surrender Value as of	12/31/2019	$145,914.65
Surrender Value as of	03/31/2019	$141,909.35

Minimum Required Cash Value as of 3/31/2019 $141,827.61

Please refer to the Definitions and Disclosures Section for further information.

Living Benefit Detail

Retirement Income Choice℠ 1.2 Issued: 12/08/2009
As of 03/31/2019

Highest Monthiversary℠ Value 5/8/2019	Withdrawal Base	Rider Withdrawal Amount	Remaining Rider Withdrawal Amount
$177,753.56	$177,753.56	$8,887.68	$6,962.79

> If you happen to own an annuity with an income rider benefit, the RMD calculations could be based upon the future value of those payments. In addition, taking income benefit withdrawals does NOT satisfy RMD requirements for your retirement accounts. You need to talk to a professional about taxes before you commit to an annuity with an income rider.

RMD's sound confusing don't they? In our above example, if your total value of the IRA's are $100,000, your total RMD on THOSE three accounts is just about $3,650. You can choose to take that amount from any combination of the three IRA's, including taking it all from one. What you can't do is take that dollar amount from your 401(k)'s.

The RMD on the $400,000 of 401(k) money equals $14,599.00. Just like the IRA accounts, you can choose to take the total 401(k) RMD amount from one or both 401(k)'s. Just as long as you get the total amount out, the IRS does not care from which 401(k) it comes. You just can't take the 401(k) RMD's from an IRA.

Sounds complicated. But the IRS also threw another rule into the mix. If you are still working and still eligible (notice we said "eligible", not necessarily contributing) to contribute to your company's 401(k) plan, you then do not have an RMD requirement at all. No RMD's required from your company-sponsored retirement plans while you are still working and eligible to contribute, even after you turn age 70.

The IRS sure didn't make this rule easy. It almost feels like they made it so complicated just so they could confuse people, especially as they get older, so that the IRS could collect penalties on incorrect RMD calculations.

Fortunately for Bill and Jean, their investment advisor suggested they work with their CPA each year to make sure they were calculating their RMD's correctly. Fortunately for Bill and Jean, they has accumulated enough assets that they really didn't need their retirement accounts to fund their retirement. And fortunately for Bill and Jean, they decided to work with a financial planning team that incorporated tax planning into the process. It was during that process that Bill and Jean remembered that for a short period of time, before they had kids, that Jean worked for a local University. While working there, she contributed to her 403(b), and like many employees, she took a "set it and forget it" approach to the retirement account.

When Bill and Jean had their tax analysis done, to determine whether it made sense to convert some portion of their retirement accounts into ROTH IRA's, it was discovered that they had never taken their RMD's from the 403(b) annuity she had through the University. After a quick calculation, it was determined that she had failed to withdraw $12,845 over the previous three years. The penalty, according to her CPA, was $6,422.50. Plus a tax bill of $2,747 for a whopping total of $9,169 in penalties and taxes.

Part IX	Additional Tax on Excess Accumulation in Qualified Retirement Plans (Including IRAs). Complete this part if you did not receive the minimum required distribution from your qualified retirement plan.	
52	Minimum required distribution for 2019 (see instructions)	52
53	Amount actually distributed to you in 2019	53
54	Subtract line 53 from line 52. If zero or less, enter -0-	54
55	**Additional tax.** Enter 50% (0.50) of line 54. Include this amount on Schedule 2 (Form 1040 or 1040-SR), line 6, or Form 1040-NR, line 57	55

Sign Here Only if You Are Filing This Form by Itself and Not With Your Tax Return

Under penalties of perjury, I declare that I have examined this form, including accompanying attachments, and to the best of my knowledge and belief, it is true, correct, and complete. Declaration of preparer (other than taxpayer) is based on all information of which preparer has any knowledge.

▶ _____ Your signature ▶ _____ Date

The solution for Bill and Jean was to request an abatement, a waiver, of the IRS penalty. Their CPA had failed to make this request, probably because Bill and Jean just handed her a 1099 from the University and the CPA didn't take any time to review the problem. She just put numbers on a page. We were able to get the IRS to waive the penalty and save the client the $6,422.50 they had already paid.

This is why tax planning matters!

What counts as truly tax-free? We have discussed the use of a ROTH and/or ROTH 401(k) extensively. There is one other tax-free option for people. If you have a weak stomach or are easily frightened, you may want to skip this approach to tax planning. Most ranking articles out there put Members of Congress, Politicians, and Lawyers at the bottom of the "trustworthy" list. Used car salesmen are frequently on that list. So are life insurance agents. Many people assume the only reason an agent sells life insurance is to get the commission associated with selling insurance. It may be true. Life insurance agents do get paid a commission when they sell a life policy. Frequently agents don't understand the policy they are selling, misrepresent how the policy works and sell insurance to people who really don't benefit from the coverage. All that adds to the negative perception of life insurance. That doesn't mean properly-structured life insurance can't be a viable tool, especially when it comes to tax planning.

Remember our Doctor who sold his practice for $3,500,000? His CPA had done the tax calculations and had given the doctor estimated tax payment coupons so he could send the IRS $986,000. That was the recommendation of the CPA – the person who the Doctor trusted to give him the best tax planning advice… "Send in a check."

Form 1040 (2018)	Frank & Sally Jones						123-45-6789		Page 2
	1	Wages, salaries, tips, etc. Attach Form(s) W-2					1	1,500,000	
Attach Form(s) W-2. Also attach Form(s) W-2G and 1099-R if tax was withheld	2a	Tax-exempt interest	2a		b	Taxable interest	2b	22,484	
	3a	Qualified dividends	3a	114,952	b	Ordinary dividends	3b	23,185	
	4a	IRAs, pensions, and annuities	4a		b	Taxable amount	4b		
	5a	Social security benefits	5a	56,825	b	Taxable amount	5b	48,301	
	6	Total income. Add lines 1 through 5. Add any amount from Schedule 1, line 22		3,500,000			6	5,093,970	
	7	Adjusted gross income. If you have no adjustments to income, enter the amount from line 6; otherwise, subtract Schedule 1, line 36, from line 6					7	5,093,970	
Standard Deduction for—	8	Standard deduction or itemized deductions (from Schedule A)					8	26,600	
• Single or married filing separately, $12,000	9	Qualified business income deduction (see instructions)					9	0	
• Married filing jointly or Qualifying widow(er), $24,000	10	Taxable income. Subtract lines 8 and 9 from line 7. If zero or less, enter -0-					10	5,067,370	
• Head of household, $18,000	11	a Tax (see inst.) 1,199,764 (check if any from: 1 ☐ Form(s) 8814 2 ☐ Form 4972 3 ☐					▶		
• If you checked any box under Standard deduction, see instructions.		b Add any amount from Schedule 2 and check here				▶ ☐	11	1,199,764	
	12	a Child tax credit/credit for other dependents ____ b Add any amount from Schedule 3 and check here ▶ ☐					12		
	13	Subtract line 12 from line 11. If zero or less, enter -0-					13	1,199,764	
	14	Other taxes. Attach Schedule 4					14	145,985	
	15	Total tax. Add lines 13 and 14					15	1,345,749	
	16	Federal income tax withheld from Forms W-2 and 1099					16		
	17	Refundable credits: a EIC (see inst.) ____ b Sch 8812 ____ c Form 8863 ____							
		Add any amount from Schedule 5					17		
	18	Add lines 16 and 17. These are your total payments					18		
Refund	19	If line 18 is more than line 15, subtract line 15 from line 18. This is the amount you overpaid					19		
Direct deposit? See instructions.	20a	Amount of line 19 you want refunded to you. If Form 8888 is attached, check here ▶ ☐					20a		
	b	Routing number ____ ▶ c Type: ☐ Checking ☐ Savings							
	d	Account number ____							
	21	Amount of line 19 you want applied to your 2019 estimated tax ▶ 21							
Amount You Owe	22	Amount you owe. Subtract line 18 from line 15. For details on how to pay, see instructions ▶					22	1,346,145	

Sale of the practice $3.5M.
Total taxes on sale and the rest of his income was $1.346M

Because tax planning matters, we created a different solution for the doctor. Remember that the doctor had made smart money choices along the way and had an ample retirement and investment portfolio to meet most of his needs. The sale of the practice would fund his legacy planning, his charitable giving, and help offset those bucket list/honey do/ and get-around-to-it items. What was the solution? Life Insurance—Properly designed cash value life insurance. The operative words here are "properly designed".

When properly designing a life insurance contract, you need to understand *what is the goal of the policy*. For some people the goal is to protect their family should they die with young children: replacing the lost income. For some, it is to pay off debt related to a mortgage. For others, it is to leave a legacy, that is, make somebody "rich". For this Doctor, the goal was three-fold: first, he wanted to leave a legacy for his kids; second, he wanted to contribute to his favorite charities; and third, he wanted to reduce his tax exposure.

The first step was to attack the current tax bill. The CPA had calculated that $986,000 tax bill. To reduce this tax bite, the solution was for him to donate $1,000,000 to a specific type of charitable trust. This allowed him to immediately write off $1,000,000 as a tax deduction. With this simple step, he was able to reduce his taxable income by $1,000,000. That in turn saved him over $350,000 in taxes.

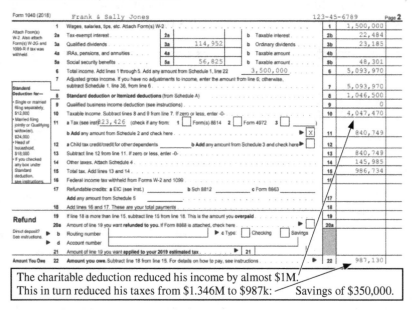

The charitable deduction reduced his income by almost $1M. This in turn reduced his taxes from $1.346M to $987k: Savings of $350,000.

The $1,000,000 went into the charitable trust and each year a portion of the in the trust goes to his charities and a portion of the trust is used to fund a $1,000,000 life insurance policy. He was able to accomplish two of his goals using one tax strategy: a lifetime of charitable giving and a legacy for his children. He was able to use what would have otherwise been spent on taxes to accomplish his goals. Every year he is able to donate more than $58,000 to charity. That makes a difference, which is what his goal was: as a doctor he made a difference in his patients' lives, and as a retiree, he is still able to make a difference in people's lives.

That is why tax planning matters!

To further eliminate his tax bill, the Doctor used a tax code, 1031, to reduce his tax bill to almost ZERO resulting from the sale of the business. IRS Code §1031 allows you to avoid taxes on the sale of property otherwise subject to capital gains by taking the proceeds from the sale and investing in substantially the same type of property within a specified period of time. In the case of the Doctor, almost $2,500,000 of the sales price he was receiving was related to the building where his practice was housed.

Form 1040 (2018)	Frank & Sally Jones			123-45-6789	Page 2
1	Wages, salaries, tips, etc. Attach Form(s) W-2			1	1,500,000
2a	Tax-exempt interest	2a	b Taxable interest	2b	22,484
3a	Qualified dividends	3a 114,952	b Ordinary dividends	3b	23,185
4a	IRAs, pensions, and annuities	4a	b Taxable amount	4b	
5a	Social security benefits	5a 56,825	b Taxable amount	5b	48,301
6	Total income. Add lines 1 through 5. Add any amount from Schedule 1, line 22	1,000,000		6	2,593,970
7	Adjusted gross income. If you have no adjustments to income, enter the amount from line 6; otherwise, subtract Schedule 1, line 36, from line 6			7	2,593,970
8	Standard deduction or itemized deductions (from Schedule A)			8	1,046,500
9	Qualified business income deduction (see instructions)			9	0
10	Taxable income. Subtract lines 8 and 9 from line 7. If zero or less, enter -0-			10	1,547,470
11	a Tax (see inst) 323,426 (check if any from: 1 ☐ Form(s) 8814 2 ☐ Form 4972 3 ☐)				
	b Add any amount from Schedule 2 and check here ▶ ☒			11	340,749
12	a Child tax credit/credit for other dependents _____ b Add any amount from Schedule 3 and check here ▶ ☐			12	
13	Subtract line 12 from line 11. If zero or less, enter -0-			13	340,749
14	Other taxes. Attach Schedule 4			14	50,985
15	Total tax. Add lines 13 and 14			15	391,734
16	Federal income tax withheld from Forms W-2 and 1099			16	
17	Refundable credits: a EIC (see inst.) _____ b Sch 8812 _____ c Form 8863 _____			17	
18	Add any amount from Schedule 5				
	Add lines 16 and 17. These are your total payments			18	
19	If line 18 is more than line 15, subtract line 15 from line 18. This is the amount you overpaid			19	
20a	Amount of line 19 you want refunded to you. If Form 8888 is attached, check here ▶ ☐			20a	
b	Routing number _____ ▶ c Type: ☐ Checking ☐ Savings				
d	Account number _____				
21	Amount of line 19 you want applied to your 2019 estimated tax ▶ 21				
22	Amount you owe. Subtract line 18 from line 15. For details on how to pay, see instructions ▶			22	392,130

> With proper planning, we were able to reduce the doctor's taxes by over $950,000. The CPA told him to send the IRS a check for $986,000; he only needed to send a check for $400,000

By using the tax codes to eliminate the doctor's tax bill, that allowed him to use the full $2.5M of his proceeds to generate $162,500 a year. And because of the way a 1031 can work, almost 40% of the income or $65,000 of the income, was tax-free. This was only the starting point for the Doctor. He wanted the $162,500, but wanted even more tax savings. Like many retirees, he didn't want to pay tax on his Social Security and quite frankly, he wanted to pay the least amount of tax legally possible. Certainly that's something most of us strive to accomplish.

He wanted to get his tax bill down and was worried about what impact RMD's at age 70 would have on his Social Security. His CPA had told him that 85% was going to be taxable and to just accept the fact that when you make considerable income, you have to pay considerable tax. We disagree. With proper planning, you can reduce and quite possibly eliminate your tax bill.

The next step in planning for the Doctor was to use life insurance, properly-structured life insurance. For five years the Doctor funded a properly-designed life insurance policy. He took the $162,500 he was receiving from his 1031 exchange and adding it to the proceeds from withdrawals from his IRA. The goal was to almost completely deplete his IRA accounts by the time he reached age 70. At the time of the sale of his practice, the doctor had about $1.5M saved in his 401(k). At retirement, he rolled his 401(k), with tax-free transfer, into an IRA.

The goal was to leave about $300,000 in the IRA and deplete the balance over the course of five years. Strategically, he withdrew $250,000 each year. He paid the taxes out of his savings accounts. Remember, from his tax return he was earning over $22,000 a year in interest, and had just under $1M in cash …earning almost nothing. It made better sense to pay taxes with those "lazy" dollars than to use his other investments that were making market returns. After taxes, combined with the 1031 income, the doctor paid a premium into a properly-designed life insurance policy, to the tune of $400,000 a year, for the full five years.

What is a properly-designed life insurance policy? A properly-designed policy (sometimes called a LIRP – Life Insurance Retirement Plan), allows for a policy owner to fund the life policy for a term of years. The policy grows based upon a contractually agreed amount: it could be a fixed interest rate, a variable interest rate or even participating in stock market returns. Based upon the returns less fees associated with owning insurance, the policy will grow to a specified amount. The beauty of life insurance is that under IRS code 7702(g) earnings in a life insurance policy are not taxable. Under IRC Section 72 any distributions are treated as a withdrawal of principle first. And finally, most life insurance contracts allow for the owner of the policy to "borrow" money from the contract and under IRC 7702 and IRC 72 such loans are not included in your taxable income. In simple English? We can get money out… tax free!

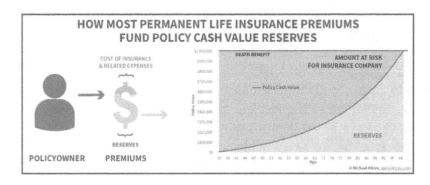

The doctor's policy was designed to front load the cash, by making excessive premium payments in the amount of $400,000 a year for five years. This in turn would allow the doctor to subsequently take tax-free withdrawals during his retirement.

Net After Tax Outlay	Annualized Surrender	Annualized Policy Loan	Annualized Loan Interest	Gross Cash Value	Total Outstanding Loan	Net Cash Value	Net Death Benefit	Reduced Paid-up Death Benefit
400,000	0	0	0	49,001	0	49,001	5,869,589	111,238
400,000	0	0	0	359,911	0	359,911	5,953,066	792,879
400,000	0	0	0	724,540	0	724,540	6,035,149	1,549,420
400,000	0	0	0	1,172,662	0	1,172,662	6,249,778	2,435,335
400,000	0	0	0	1,664,543	0	1,664,543	6,505,427	3,358,778
-162,000†	0	524,398	0	2,130,457	524,398	1,586,952	6,141,022	3,113,380
-162,000†	0	543,506	19,108	2,614,199	1,067,904	1,504,088	5,755,713	2,870,946
-162,000†	0	566,605	42,207	3,121,885	1,634,509	1,421,089	5,348,876	2,640,743
-162,000†	0	590,686	66,287	3,656,391	2,225,195	1,339,805	4,924,460	2,425,295
-162,000†	0	615,790	91,391	4,220,739	2,840,984	1,262,192	4,485,964	2,226,796
-162,000†	0	279,563	117,563	4,444,533	3,120,547	1,194,542	4,388,734	2,054,773
-162,000†	0	291,444	129,444	4,641,991	3,411,991	1,121,170	4,280,349	1,881,095
-162,000†	0	303,830	141,830	4,906,671	3,715,821	1,036,107	4,160,471	1,696,117
-162,000†	0	316,743	154,743	5,151,435	4,032,564	950,667	4,029,103	1,519,098
-162,000†	0	330,205	168,205	5,403,786	4,362,769	858,779	3,886,021	1,340,147
-162,000†	0	344,238	182,238	5,735,824	4,707,007	831,948	3,841,202	1,268,833
-162,000†	0	358,868	196,868	6,088,930	5,065,875	810,934	3,799,213	1,209,574
-162,000†	0	374,120	212,120	6,463,712	5,439,996	795,696	3,759,030	1,161,414
-162,000†	0	390,020	228,020	6,855,050	5,830,016	780,435	3,720,034	1,115,389
-162,000†	0	406,596	244,596	7,274,089	6,236,613	776,499	3,681,237	1,087,230

The policy was designed for the doctor to make 5 payments of $400,000. In the 6th year, the doctor was able to withdraw $162,000 a year, TAX FREE!

By designing the policy correctly, the cash value was maximized in order to provide tax-free income to the doctor, and the death benefit was reduced down to the smallest amount possible – while allowing the policy to still distribute the $162,000 to the doctor. With an expected life expectancy of 90 years of age, the doctor will have invested approximately $2M into the policy, and upon his death at age 90 he will have withdrawn over $3.8M tax free, and still have a death benefit going to his heirs of over $1.1M.

It is important to understand how the cash values, death benefits, and policy loans all work together to ensure that you don't end up violating IRC Sections 7702 and 72, which would result in everything coming unraveled and a huge tax bill.

That is why tax planning matters!

When a well-planned, tax efficient, retirement plan comes together:

Income:

Social Security		$ 56,825
Dividends and Interest		47,571
1031 Income	$162,500	162,500
40% tax free	65,000	
Taxable	97,500	
IRA Distributions		10,949
Capital Gains		41,823
Total Income		$319,668

Taxes: **ZERO! NONE! NOTHING!**

| Form 1040 (2018) | Frank & Sally Jones | | | | 123-45-6789 | | Page 2 |

	1	Wages, salaries, tips. etc. Attach Form(s) W-2				1	
Attach Form(s) W-2. Also attach Form(s) W-2G and 1099-R if tax was withheld.	2a	Tax-exempt interest	2a		b Taxable interest	2b	8,469
	3a	Qualified dividends	3a	36,252	b Ordinary dividends	3b	2,850
	4a	IRAs, pensions, and annuities	4a		b Taxable amount	4b	10,949
	5a	Social security benefits	5a	56,825	b Taxable amount	5b	48,301
	6	Total income. Add lines 1 through 5. Add any amount from Schedule 1, line 22 139,323				6	209,892
Standard Deduction for—	7	Adjusted gross income. If you have no adjustments to income, enter the amount from line 6; otherwise, subtract Schedule 1, line 36, from line 6				7	209,892
• Single or married filing separately. $12,000	8	Standard deduction or itemized deductions (from Schedule A)				8	133,000
• Married filing jointly or Qualifying widow(er), $24,000	9	Qualified business income deduction (see instructions)				9	0
	10	Taxable income. Subtract lines 8 and 9 from line 7. If zero or less, enter -0-				10	76,892
• Head of household, $18,000	11	a Tax (see inst)_____ (check if any from: 1 ☐ Form(s) 8814 2 ☐ Form 4972 3 ☐)					
• If you checked any box under Standard deduction, see instructions.		b Add any amount from Schedule 2 and check here			▶☐	11	
	12	a Child tax credit/credit for other dependents_____ b Add any amount from Schedule 3 and check here▶☐				12	
	13	Subtract line 12 from line 11. If zero or less, enter -0-				13	
	14	Other taxes. Attach Schedule 4				14	
	15	Total tax. Add lines 13 and 14				15	
	16	Federal income tax withheld from Forms W-2 and 1099				16	
	17	Refundable credits: a EIC (see inst.)_____ b Sch 8812_____ c Form 8863_____					
		Add any amount from Schedule 5_____				17	
	18	Add lines 16 and 17. These are your total payments				18	
Refund	19	If line 18 is more than line 15, subtract line 15 from line 18. This is the amount you overpaid				19	
	20a	Amount of line 19 you want refunded to you. If Form 8888 is attached, check here			▶☐	20a	
Direct deposit? See instructions	▶b	Routing number			▶c Type: ☐ Checking ☐ Savings		
	▶d	Account number					
	21	Amount of line 19 you want applied to your 2019 estimated tax ▶ 21					
Amount You Owe	22	Amount you owe. Subtract line 18 from line 15. For details on how to pay, see instructions			▶	22	
	23	Estimated tax penalty (see instructions) ▶ 23					

Remember that a portion of the 1031 income is tax free and therefore does not show up on the tax return.

So what happens to this doctor when the taxes rates go up, like so many have predicted they will?

If taxes rates double in the future, the doctor still remains in the zero percent tax bracket.

Tax Planning Matters!

THE SECURE ACT OF 2019

As of Dec. 20, 2019, President Trump signed **THE SECURE ACT** into law. The changes contained in the Act may have an impact on your retirement plan, but most certainly will have an impact on your tax-planning choices.

Here are a few key takeaways to consider:

I. **Required Minimum Distributions:** We discussed those pesky RMD's and with **THE SECURE ACT,** you have a little breathing room on when you are required to start taking your distributions and giving one-third of your proceeds to the IRS. Remember, at age 70½, you were being forced to take a distribution from your retirement accounts. You had to take this money out each and every year, regardless if you needed it or not. You had all those crazy calculations on all those different accounts and if you missed something, just by happenchance, the IRS wanted to penalize you 50% PLUS they wanted the taxes.

What has changed is that you no longer have to take money out of your retirement accounts by age 70½: now you have to take the money out by age 72. You basically get a one-and-one-half year postponement of your RMDs. This could provide a key cushion when it comes to your income needs, especially if your first RMD would have been in a year when the stock markets were in decline. While there is a small positive from this, all the other issues remain:

which account to take from, what percentage to take, how to calculate on the various investment accounts, and all the other issues that arise when trying to avoid the 50% penalty.

II. **Contribution Age Limits:** With **THE SECURE ACT** in place, for those who work past the age of 70, you are allowed to contribute into your IRA, even if you are otherwise required to take a RMD. With Americans living and working longer, this can be a huge boost. You will still have RMD's, but if you move your existing IRA's into your existing 401(k)'s, you may not be subject to much of an RMD at all.

And remember, if you have a spouse who is retired, you will now be able to contribute to their IRA's. You can still use this contribution to create a "back-door" ROTH contribution if your income otherwise prevents a direct contribution to a ROTH.

III. **Part-Time Coverage:** If you do choose to continue working past age 72, when RMD's now come into play, you may be eligible to participate in your company's 401(k) plan. The problem is that in the past, you probably had to work at least X amount of hours per year in order to qualify for participation. For many plans, this required you to work at least 1000 hours a year. Not hard to do if you choose to work 20 hrs. per week year around. For many of those who want to continue to work in some capacity, those hours might be hard to hit. The new rule, under **THE SECURE ACT**, provides for participation with just 500 hours a year, that is about 10 hrs. per week. Remember, your ability to participate in your company's plan is key to avoiding current year RMDs.

One of the new rules is actually quite interesting and could cause incredible problems in the investment world.

For insurance agents and financial advisors who sell annuities with income riders as part of their practice, the new rule requiring 401(k) plan administrators to show on the 401(k) statement how much a participant could receive if the TOTAL account balance was used to purchase an annuity, is a validation of their long-held belief that if you need income during retirement, an annuity is a viable tool.

The problem is that most firms and insurance companies that provide annuities have an unwritten guideline, a rule, that limits the amount of money an advisor can actually put into an annuity on behalf of their client. For many firms and advisors, this amount is no more than 50% of the client's investments should be held in an annuity.

LIFETIME INCOME DISCLOSURE STATEMENTS

The regulatory agency for security licensed advisors is called FINRA. They have a guidebook they provide to investors considering using annuities: *https://www.finra.org/investors/insights/your-guide-annuities-introduction.*

For insurance agents, the National Association of Insurance Commissioners (State Insurance Commissioners) have also produced a guidebook that might prove useful in your research: *https://www.naic.org/documents/prod_serv_consumer_anb_la.pdf.*

The idea here is that the 401(k) participant uses the value of their 401(k) to produce income. This makes sense because for the most part, people who put money away into their employer retirement accounts are typically doing so to save for their retirement. The goal they have is to save enough money in these accounts so that when they retire, they have enough income to enjoy their retirement years. So it makes sense that the 401(k) administrators should tell their participants how much they could expect to receive if they took income from their retirement plans.

The concern about this new feature, showing the possible income for the participant, is that the income is based upon what is called a SPIA: a Single Premium Immediate Annuity. This means that the number being shown in our example, $1,263 per month, is for the life of JUST THE PARTICIPANT. It is based upon a single life. This means if you are married, your spouse would not get any income or have any assets available from the plan should you die first. That is right, once you pass away, the income is gone. You have basically turned the value of the retirement plan over to an insurance company and they in turn have guaranteed YOU a lifetime of income. If you live 100 years, you did great. If you get hit by that proverbial pickle truck the day after your first check, there is nothing left. ZERO. Nothing. It is gone.

Now it is true that you will probably have options on whether to put the whole amount into an annuity, whether to take a single life and get the maximum value out of the amount, or to provide for your spouse and receive a lesser amount. The choices will be similar to that of when you have a company-sponsored pension plan. The options are almost overwhelming, and you will need to pay attention so that you do not inadvertently cut off your spouse or heirs.

Other Provisions: These include (a) allowing grad students to use their stipends and grants to qualify as income for contribution purposes, (b) foster care providers and adult care givers will also have opportunities to contribute based upon their payments, (c) employers will now offer "automatic" enrollment to employees, requiring employees to opt out of saving for retirement, and (d) incentives for small businesses to set up plans for their employees.

As always, there can't only be good news, right?

Stretch Provisions Eliminated: As we have previously discussed, any assets left inside a retirement account left to a spouse had one set of rules related to required minimum distributions. Basically the spouse was allowed to continue taking the RMD's based upon their age when they inherited the account. For children and other heirs, there was a different lifetime table, but effectively they were also able to stretch that amount left in the retirement account over their own lifetimes.

This is important because for many heirs, they are in their peak-earning years and they may not want to be forced to take out more income from their inherited IRA's. It only forces them to pay more taxes on money they don't really need at this point. Sounds familiar? One of the many reasons to consider converting to a ROTH IRA, right?

Well, perhaps. The new rule eliminates the ability of a non-spouse beneficiary to stretch out those withdrawals over their lifetime. This means that non-spouse heirs will no longer be allowed to stretch out those withdrawals, which in turn means that those tax-free/tax-deferred accounts are not able to grow tax-free/deferred over their lives. They lose the ability to let those accounts grow for decades without having to pay tax on any current tax on potential growth.

Now, with few exceptions, non-spousal beneficiaries are now required to withdraw 100% of the inherited account within 10 years. This means that if you have a 401(k), IRA, or other employer sponsored retirement account, your heirs will have to take 100% of that money out, add it to their own current income, and pay taxes on it – each and every year for up to 10 years. This is a huge loss of potential tax-free growth and income for your heirs.

With every problem comes potential solutions. The changes to the stretch accounts is no different. Clearly the conversion to a ROTH IRA is more important now than ever. While it is true that an *inherited* ROTH account has the same 10-year withdrawal requirement, at least those withdrawals are tax free. With proper tax planning during the withdrawal period, those ROTH assets can be converted into either tax-free assets for the future or can be converted into tax-efficient assets in the future.

Tax efficient? Think about our Warren Buffet approach. Upon the withdrawal of the ROTH assets, if your heir were to invest those in assets that produce only capital gains, then your heir would have the opportunity to have that growth and dividend income exposed to favorable tax rates. Remember, if structured correctly, capital gains rates can be as low as ZERO. That is correct, the benefit of having a ROTH is that any withdrawals results in ZERO taxes. The same can be true if your heir(s) properly structure(s) their ROTH withdrawals.

While we think the Warren Buffet approach to capital gains and taxes is important (remember, capital gains are currently taxed between ZERO and 15%, while ordinary income is taxed up to almost 40% when you include the additional Medicare taxes), the reality is that they can change capital gains rates, as we have seen over the last couple decades (capital gains rates have been as high as 28% and as low as 0% over the last 20 years). What hasn't changed in decades is the ability to receive tax-free income from properly-structured life insurance.

That means while tax efficient is good: tax free is even better. The whole purpose of the ROTH IRA was to allow your beneficiaries (assuming your children) to take the balance of that inherited account over their lifetime. Let's say you have managed to accumulate a ROTH account with $1M. Under the old rules, when your daughter inherited that account upon your death, she was allowed to take the $1M out over her lifetime, about 5% per year. This allowed the money to continue to grow tax free while still providing income for her. If your daughter died with money left in that ROTH account, her kids were allowed to continue taking that money out tax free. It was a wonderful tax planning strategy.

At first glance, it appears that **THE SECURE ACT** has taken away the ability to continue growth tax free for our heirs. **THE SECURE ACT** requires your non-spousal beneficiary to withdraw 100% of the ROTH account (or IRA acct.) by the end of ten years. In doing so, it forces the money in that ROTH/ IRA out of tax-deferred growth into an account that, minimally, would be subject to capital gains tax.

But with a little tax planning, your beneficiaries can continue to grow their inheritance tax free and create tax-free income. Remember, your daughter was forced to take required minimum distributions from the ROTH, i.e., creating income. Now, instead of taking 5% (or deferring the whole thing for 10 years and taking a lump sum), what if she took out 10% per year and purchased a life insurance policy?

Let's take a look at that $1M ROTH IRA. Let's assume a few things: Your daughter inherits the ROTH at age 50 and wants to retire at age 60. She will need income during her retirement, so she will take the money out of the ROTH over 7 years (we'll explain why 7 years is key), the money grows at 5%, and finally, combined Federal and State tax rates are 22%.

When your daughter, Susan, takes her withdrawal every year, she will be putting the money into an investment account and be required to pay taxes on her capital gains and dividends each year. If she were to inherit the $1M from your ROTH IRA and take $164,590 per year for 7 years and earn 5% on her investments,

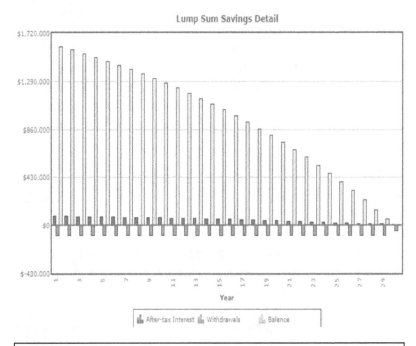

Lump Sum Savings Detail

After-tax Interest   Withdrawals   Balance

HOW LONG WILL MY MONEY LAST WITH SYSTEMATIC WITHDRAWALS?
Starting Balance:
  $1,630,000
  5% Rate of Return
  22% Tax Bracket
  Yearly Distributions
  Total Distributions over 30 years will be approximately $2.75M

then her account would have grown to about $1.63M, after taxes. Taking this tax-efficient approach, she would be able to withdraw about $7,750 a month for thirty years and have nothing left for her heirs.

Sounds pretty reasonable. Susan is able to supplement her income needs for 30 years with an additional $7,750 a month income. That seems pretty tax efficient.

Perhaps a better approach would be using a tax-free strategy. Making the exact same assumptions, Susan could increase her income to $10,178 per month TAX FREE, and still have $1.2M available to her heirs, also Tax Free. You're probably asking yourself, how is that possible?

Susan chose to use the Ed Slott approach to retirement planning: she chose to use the benefits of life insurance. By taking the same $164,590 withdrawals as before, Susan put those tax-free proceeds into a properly-designed life insurance contract. She took the same 7 years of withdrawals, and each and every year, she "invested" in her life insurance contract instead of the stock market via her brokerage account. The benefit here is that Susan adds no risk to her investments as a properly-designed life insurance policy does not expose her to stock market volatility. In addition to removal of the ups and downs of the stock market, she is also sheltered from paying taxes on her dividends and capital gains. In properly-structured life insurance, there are no taxes on any gains, dividends, or interest.

Properly structured is important. In order to be properly structured, you must do a few things. First, you must fund your life insurance premiums in such a fashion to avoid what is called an MEC, or a Modified Endowment Contract. In the simplest terms, an MEC translates into "taxable" when you take withdrawals from your insurance contract. With a properly-structured contract, you can always "borrow" the gains and withdraw the principle. Borrowed money is never taxable and neither is your principle. You must also use a policy that is designed to create income, that is, you want to maximize your income options, not necessarily your death benefit options.

In this scenario, the goal for Susan's parents was for Susan to have the money for her to use over her lifetime. Susan didn't need the money until she retires at age 60, so being forced to take all the money out of the ROTH IRA isn't really in her best interests, but with the new Secure Act rules, she must make sure the inherited ROTH is drained of all assets by the end of ten years.

End of Year	Beg/ End of Yr Age	Annualized Annual Premium	Dist. Amount
1	50/51	$164,590.00	$0
2	51/52	$164,590.00	$0
3	52/53	$164,590.00	$0
4	53/54	$164,590.00	$0
5	54/55	$164,590.00	$0
		$822,950.00	$0
6	55/56	$164,590.00	$0
7	56/57	$164,590.00	$0
8	57/58	$0.00	$0
9	58/59	$0.00	$0
10	59/60	$0.00	$0
		$1,152,130.00	$0
11	60/61	$0.00	$122,136
12	61/62	$0.00	$122,136
13	62/63	$0.00	$122,136
14	63/64	$0.00	$122,136
15	64/65	$0.00	$122,136

In this illustration you can see that Susan took her $164,590 per year and paid the premium on the properly-structured cash value life insurance policy.

At age 60, when Susan is ready to retire, she can start taking $122,136 a year out to supplement her income.

In addition to the LIFETIME income provided by this properly-designed life insurance, like all life insurance, there is a death benefit for Susan's heirs.

With the tax-efficient approach, at the end of ten years, Susan had about $1.625M to leave to her heirs should she die unexpectedly. By using the tax-free approach, if Susan were to die unexpectedly at age 60, she would be leaving her heirs slightly more than $4.1M. And keep in mind that the money she is leaving is 100% tax free as well.

You can see that the death benefit decreases after the 10th year. Why? That is because Susan starting taking her tax free withdrawals of $122k per year. Just like withdrawals in her brokerage account would result in depleting the account over time, taking withdrawals from your life insurance policy will have similar consequences. The difference is that with the properly designed life insurance, Susan will have tax free income plus when she passes away, there is still a substantial legacy.

Notice below that by the time Susan dies at age 90, she will have withdrawn over $3.6M from her policy and still leave a legacy of the original $1M she inherited in the ROTH IRA forty years ago!

Clearly Tax Planning Matters!

Account Value	Surrender Value	Death Benefit
$143,848	$0	$4,151,482
$294,746	$150,794	$4,151,482
$454,282	$317,906	$4,151,482
$624,057	$502,833	$4,151,482
$804,861	$698,791	$4,151,482
$997,552	$906,635	$4,151,482
$1,202,693	$1,126,928	$4,151,482
$1,253,494	$1,192,882	$4,151,482
$1,306,508	$1,261,049	$4,151,482
$1,361,941	$1,331,635	$4,151,482
$1,443,828	$1,318,097	$4,025,750
$1,530,406	$1,272,052	$3,893,128
$1,621,863	$1,223,619	$3,753,239
$1,720,283	$1,174,484	$3,605,683
$1,826,287	$1,124,847	$3,450,042

While this approach, using properly-designed life insurance has been addressed in this book, a couple great resources for more information on using life insurance as part of your tax-free retirement planning can be found in Patrick Kelly's national best seller "Tax-Free Retirement" and by retirement guru, CPA, and bestselling author, America's IRA Expert, Ed Slot. His book, *The Retirement Savings Time Bomb ...and How To Defuse It* is a retirement guidebook for many tax professionals.

Tax Planning Does Matter!

CHAPTER 7

BONUS SECTION: SMALL BUSINESS & SMALL BUSINESS OWNERS

In some of the examples we gave, we talked about different kinds of income and professions. When thinking about workers, we sometimes think about the big tech, insurance, or retail companies.

However, the reality is that most people don't work for big corporate America. In fact, according to the Census Bureau, there are about 5.6 million employers in the United States and almost all firms with less than 20 employees make up about 89% of those employers.[15] This means that the average American works for a small employer. These types of workers are the backbone of our economy, and thus, they need a little extra attention when it comes to saving taxes.

As an individual, small business owners and their employees can employ all the tax planning strategies we have previously discussed. But there are a few other options and bits of information that the small business owner should consider:

O Many small business owners offer their employees the ability to participate in a company-sponsored retirement plan called

---

15. https://sbecouncil.org/about-us/facts-and-data/

a SEP IRA. A Simplified Employee Pension is a basic and simple way for an employer to contribute to their employee's retirement as well as their own retirement plans.

They are simple because they are easy to open – as easy as opening an IRA – and because they have very simple rules when it comes to contributing to them:

- must be 21 years old
- must have worked for the employer for at least 3 out of the last 5 years
- must have at least $600 in compensation per...

Once established, the employer can contribute up to 25% of his/her profit into his own plan. The downside is that whatever percentage of your profit/salary you contribute to your own plan, you must make that much of a contribution to your employee's SEP plan.

All contributions are tax deductible for the employer. Note that the employee does not make a contribution to the SEP. The employee can however, open their own IRA or ROTH and make contributions based upon their income level.

o An employer can also provide a 401(k) program for their employees: a defined contribution plan. It is called a defined contribution because the rules dictate how much can be contributed by the employee participant and the employer. The employee takes on the risk of success or failure in having the right amount of money saved in order to fund their retirement.

These plans are a little more complicated for the small business owner and do required annual tax filing via an IRA form 5500. This form is required when a company-sponsored retirement plan has more than $500,000 in assets. This means as the retirement accounts grow in value over time, through market growth or contributions, you may be required to file additional tax forms for your company plan. Where they come in handy is for the very small firm, say two or three employees including the owner and his/her spouse. This is when the 401(k) can be a very creative solution to tax planning.

The costs of setting up an annual administration can be intimidating at first. For example, hiring a third-party administrator tasked with setting up the plan may cost several thousand dollars. Annual reporting can cost just as much. Some payroll companies will offset the setup costs or waive them altogether.

The basic rules are as follows:

- Can restrict age participating to those older than 21
- Can restrict when they can start participating: usually within a year
- Employees/Employers can contribute 100% of their salary up to annual contribution limits: Currently in 2020 $19,500 for those under age 50, with an additional $6,500 catch up allowed for those 50 and over
- Employer can set up a 401(k), ROTH 401(k), or both
- Safe Harbor contributions avoid top-heavy testing
- Can provide profit sharing

For the employer, especially a person who is the only "employee" of the firm, the amount that can be set aside is fairly substantial. However, if there are other employees involved, an employer will need to pass a "top-heavy" test: a test to make sure that the highly compensated aren't the only ones participating in the 401(k). The way around this rule is called a "safe harbor" provision. The safe harbor provision requires the employer to "match" any contributions the employee makes. The match, typically dollar-for-dollar for the first 3% and then 50 cents per dollar for the next 2%. This basically means if the employee contributes 5% of their wages, the employer will need to contribute to that employee's 401(k) another 4% of the employee wages.

Jim Salary: $50,000
401(k) Contribution: __2,500__ (5% of his salary)*
Jim's W2 taxable wages: $47,500

---

*This is a salary deferral and goes into Jim's 401(k) (or if ROTH 401(k), there would be no reduction in Jim's taxable wages). In addition to Jim's contribution, the employer would also be required to contribute $2,500 to Jim's 401(k) plan.

YOUR EMPLOYEE PRE-TAX DEFERRAL Vesting = 100.00% / Your Vested Balance is $155,828.19

Fund Option	Beginning Balance	Contributions	Exchanges	Withdrawals	Gain/Loss	Adjustments	Closing Balance	Units
Balanced								
Vngrd Trgt Rtrmt 2025 Inv	$108,952.13	$5,731.28	$0.00	$0.00	$1,203.10	$3,126.45	$119,012.96	76.558.6528
Vngrd Trgt Rtrmt 2040 Inv	$587.39	$0.00	$0.00	$0.00	$2.49	$0.00	$589.88	356.0636
Sub Total	$109,539.52	$5,731.28	$0.00	$0.00	$1,205.59	$3,126.45	$119,602.84	
Outstanding Loan Balance							$36,225.35	
Total	$109,539.52	$5,731.28	$0.00	$0.00	$1,205.59	$3,126.45	$155,828.19	

YOUR EMPLOYER MATCHING Vesting = 100.00% / Your Vested Balance is $30,148.12

Fund Option	Beginning Balance	Contributions	Exchanges	Withdrawals	Gain/Loss	Adjustments	Closing Balance	Units
Balanced								
Vngrd Trgt Rtrmt 2025 Inv	$28,577.77	$1,071.23	$0.00	$0.00	$304.86	$0.00	$29,953.86	19.268.7195
Vngrd Trgt Rtrmt 2040 Inv	$193.44	$0.00	$0.00	$0.00	$0.82	$0.00	$194.26	117.2606
Sub Total	$28,771.21	$1,071.23	$0.00	$0.00	$305.68	$0.00	$30,148.12	
Total	$28,771.21	$1,071.23	$0.00	$0.00	$305.68	$0.00	$30,148.12	

This example shows a yearly employee contribution of $5,731.28. In addition, the employer must make a matching contribution. Notice there is a "vesting" of 100%. In this example, the employee has vested 100% in the matching contribution. The employer can require up to 5 years to vest in any match.

Where the real opportunity comes is in the case of a person who is the only full-time employee of the company. In another example, many doctors and dentists may have numerous nurses, practitioners, hygienists, and administrative help, but in many circumstances, those employees are not eligible to participate because of hours worked or income needs.

Just consider the comparison between a SEP and a 401(k) for a dentist with no eligible employees. The dentist makes $100,000 a year and takes the standard deduction:

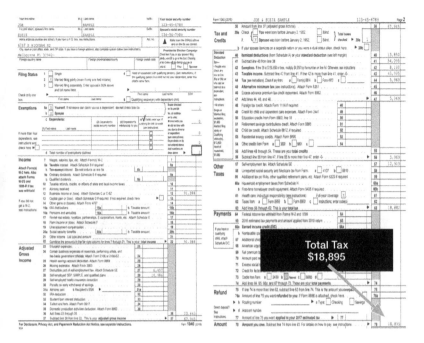

The Dentist is able to put away 25% of his "salary", in this example, the salary is represented by the profit in the practice. The total tax bill in this scenario, with self-employment and income tax, is about $19,000. The dentist is able to put about $17,000 into a SEP.

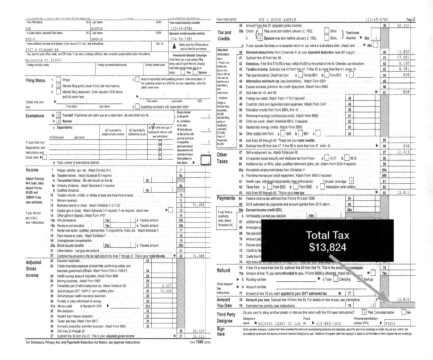

With a little more tax planning, here is the exact same professional with the exact same income:

By using a 401(k) with a profit-sharing option, we were able to set aside almost $40,000 more for retirement plus we reduced the tax exposure by 25%. More money in your pocket and less money going to pay taxes. Definitely a win-win situation.

If we went the next step and offered a traditional defined benefit plan, that is, a pension, the amount of money that can be saved is incredible. A defined benefit is different from a defined contribution in that the defined benefit sets the amount of income a participant will receive during retirement. For example, some Federal Employees have a retirement benefit that pays 2% of their last three year's salary, per year of work. This means that if the employee worked for 40 years, their pension would be 80% of their salary. There are a few more rules involved with this calculation, but it serves as an example of how a defined benefit

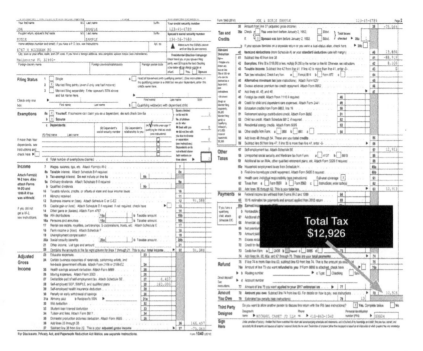

While the tax savings difference is nominal, the amount that is contributed to the retirement accounts has gone from about $19,000 in a SEP, to about $54,000 in a 401(k), and now with a defined benefit plan, we are able to increase that contribution to $160,000. That is a substantial amount being saved towards retirement.

Additionally, the example provided here actually results in a loss on the tax return. Remember that the income was only $100,000 and yet the dentist was able to save $160,000. That means that the tax return will have a substantial loss on the return. In this case, there is a loss being reported in the amount of $75,000. The dentist could then convert $75,000 of an existing IRA into a ROTH and pay ZERO taxes.

In fact, it could be possible to get almost $60,000 into a ROTH 401(k), almost another $160,000 going into a defined benefit, create a loss on the return, and have another $75,000 converted from an IRA to a ROTH.

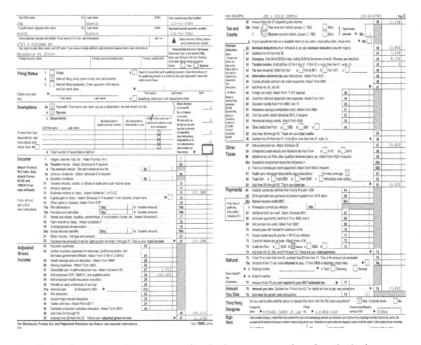

Let's look at another example, let's assume the dentist's income isn't $100,000, but is $300,000 instead. Using a combination of tax planning techniques including a defined benefit, a defined contribution, and an employee welfare program, the dentist is able to put away almost $225,000 towards retirement, and with a $300,000 income, the total tax bill is less than $20,000.

What exactly is an "employee welfare benefit plan"? This is very specific plan under 419(e) of the Internal Revenue Code. The plan allows an employee to set aside money to provide for retirement benefits covering such things as life insurance, HEALTH INSURANCE, LONG TERM CARE, and other medical expenses that arise after retirement. Imagine being able to use tax-deferred accounts to pay for your health care costs as you go through retirement AND the ability to leave a legacy to your heirs via life insurance.

Plus, when planning is done correctly, the cash value of the life insurance policy can be extracted from the plan and provide additional tax-free income during retirement.

Bottom line, think about this for a minute, for a dentist (or any professional) who makes $300,000 in profits, the typical tax bill would be almost $100,000. Because she took time to sit down with a tax planner, not only did the dentist reduce their taxes by $80,000, they also were able to save almost $225,000 for their retirement.

That is why tax planning matters, even for Business Owners.

At the end of the day, it doesn't matter how much you make, it is how much you keep. By taking the time to understand taxes and how they impact you today as well in retirement, you will give yourself the greatest opportunity to live life paying the least amount of taxes legally possible.

Your first step was reading this book. But that is only the beginning. Now you must use the knowledge you have gained to find the right advice giver. You need to find an advisor that is not only well versed in retirement planning but also in tax planning. You should ask them plenty of questions: we provided you with a list which is a good starting point.

Don't let this information discourage you. It may take time to find the right advice as the field of those who understand both tax and investment planning is fairly narrow. It is further complicated by the number of CPA's and Investment advisors who market themselves as tax planners, but don't really go beyond the basics when it comes to getting you to the ZERO tax bracket.

That advisor should be able to show you their strategy to get you to the ZERO tax bracket. They should be able to tell you exactly how much should be in the taxable bucket. They should be able to calculate how much of your taxable bucket will be subject to ordinary tax rates and how much will be subject to capital gains rates. Remember, a properly-structured asset allocation will result in your capital gains being in the ZERO percent tax bracket.

The advisor should be able to give you a step-by-step guide showing you exactly how much of your retirement accounts should be converted into tax-free ROTH accts as well as how many years will it take in order to break even on the cost of the conversion. Remember, you will pay taxes on the conversion and the cost of those taxes are part of the calculation when it comes to a ROTH conversion.

Finally, the advice should include whether you should use properly-designed life insurance in your retirement plan. The benefits of using a properly-designed policy are numerous: ability to use the death benefit to cover the high costs associated with long-term-care and the need for a nursing home; the ability to leave a legacy or to supplement the loss of pension income or social security upon your death, and finally (and arguably most importantly), is the ability to create an additional bucket of tax-free income for you and your heirs.

Once you have found that right person, you can begin your journey towards a tax-free retirement. At that point, it won't matter if the government raises taxes in the future. When you are in the zero percent tax bracket, tax rates do not matter.

Paying zero taxes can't be a bad thing.

That is why tax planning matters.

CHAPTER 8

IN CONCLUSION – SUMMARY

In previous sections, we outlined many details by example of tax strategies, and why taxes matter. One effective way to prove out these examples and truly comprehend the realm of possibilities is using the three basic tax buckets. Those three basic tax buckets are:

1. **Taxable**
2. **Tax-Deferred**
3. **Tax Free**

Now that you have read this book, which one do you think your money should be in?

PUT IN THE TAX BUCKETS!

There is a mathematically ideal amount of money to have in each bucket. Your goal should be to have three to six months of expenses set aside in safe and secure money for emergencies. This will be in a **Taxable bucket**. You may also consider having additional resources set aside in a taxable bucket, but you will want to make sure that the bucket is subject to capital gains taxes, not ordinary tax rates. This is the Warren Buffet rule: never pay a higher tax rate than a clerical worker!

Your **Tax-deferred bucket** should hold no more money than would cause your Social Security to be taxable when taking your required minimum distributions. This means that your RMD's should be less than about the $12,000 for singles and $24,000 for married filing jointly that is available as a standard deduction in 2020.

If the goal is to keep your RMD's under the standard deduction, then an ideal amount in these accounts should be somewhere between $150,000 and $300,000. Of course, you will need to calculate how the RMD will impact your Social Security. Ultimately you want no more in your retirement accounts so that when you add your RMD's into your income, you do not cause your Social Security to be taxable.

The balance of your money should be in the **Tax-free bucket**: ROTH IRA's, ROTH 401(k)'s, and Properly-Designed Cash Value Life Insurance.

By following this approach of tax efficiency, you will not be in a place where you worry that the government may raise taxes in the future. If you have designed your retirement income plan properly and have funded your money buckets correctly, you will live a retirement of tax-free income.

They say that there are two things in life you can't avoid: Death and Taxes. While these are words of wisdom and have been uttered down through the generations, this book has given you the necessary information so you may be able to at least avoid taxes.

It is well known that here in the United States of America, tax avoidance is legal, but tax evasion is not. Tax evasion opens offenders to criminal charges. You very likely have heard of the famous case that supports the legal description of tax avoidance philosophy.

We now add those oft-quoted lines from the most recognizable tax judgment for *all* American taxpayers handed down by Judge Learned Hand:

"Anyone may arrange his affairs so that his taxes shall be as low as possible; he is not bound to choose that pattern which best pays the treasury. There is not even a patriotic duty to increase one's taxes. Over and over again the Courts have said that there is nothing sinister in so arranging affairs as to keep taxes as low as possible. Everyone does it, rich and poor alike and all do right, for nobody owes any public duty to pay more than the law demands."

Judge Learned Hand
Judge, U. S. Court of Appeals

As quoted in:
Gregory v. Helvering 69 F.2d 809, 810 (2d Cir. 1934), aff'd, 293 U.S. 465, 55 S.Ct. 266, 79 L.Ed. 596 (1935)

In the simplest terms, broken down, there is nothing wrong with structuring your assets, your income, and your estate to reduce or eliminate the need to pay income taxes. Reading this book is the first step towards having a completely tax-free retirement.

Overall, making these kinds of investment in your future takes commitment, expertise, and support. As you have learned in the pages of this book, tax planning matters! This overall change takes time and it takes planning. However, with the information in this book, you now have the tools and knowledge in order to make smart money choices as well as smart tax choices.

What you do next is yours to do.

Art McPherson & Michael Canet, JD, LLM

Their combined firms, McPherson Financial Group and the Prostatis Group, a Registered Investment Advisor, have over $500,000,000 under their management team. They are exclusive boutique planning firms that specialize in comprehensive financial planning services and retirement income planning. Their process takes the necessary time to understand your individual financial needs and putting together financial programs designed to meet those needs. Their advisors have a fiduciary relationship with their clients and look out for their clients' best interest.

About Art

Arthur "Art" McPherson is a leading financial professional and advisor, contributing to articles, radio shows, and publications over his past 28 years in the industry. Arthur works closely with a variety of clients and organizations while also sharing his financial framework with his community and clients. Art is a current host of the radio program, "The Art of Money Radio," which can be heard on iHeartRadio and WMMB 1240 or 1350 AM and WFLA 100.7 FM radio, or streaming online at: www.iheart.com.

As a finance veteran, Arthur's experience, education and philosophy have allowed him to develop a unique money method. He uses this formula to help his clients reach their goals and support a stress-free and prosperous retirement. Using a variety of platforms, Arthur shares his perspective and learnings with Americans on the best ways to prepare for retirement.

Arthur is also the co-author of the book, *Nothing is Certain But Death and Taxes...Until Now!!*. You can find Arthur's articles in various publications in print and online, including *Forbes, Fortune, Fox Business* websites. Arthur began in the financial industry in 1993, he co-formed The McPherson Group with his father, and added financial services to Dave McPherson and Associates in 1995. Today, he is the current president of McPherson Financial Group, managing over 200 million in assets for their clients.

Arthur graduated from Florida State University College of Business with a Bachelor of Science in Marketing. He received his LUTCF® designation from The American College and the National Association of Insurance and Financial Advisors. Arthur is also licensed as a representative of World Equity Group, Inc., as well as a Registered Investment Advisor with Prostatis Group. All entities mentioned within are separate entities, and are not owned or controlled by World Equity Group, Inc. He sits on both Formula Folios Advisory Board, which manages over $3 Billion in assets, as well as The Financial Independence Council, which provides education in an effort to make financial security a cornerstone for every American family.

Arthur is grateful to call the beautiful state of Florida home. Between work and family life, he finds great enjoyment in antique cars, boating, and motorcycling. Arthur is a muscle-car collector and enthusiastic sports fan who appreciates the sense of community these hobbies provide him and his family. In addition to watching gameday events at home, Arthur is an active board member and a booster for Florida State University, and can often be found at FSU home games tailgating before the big game with his family and friends.

For more info:
- https://mcphersonfg.com/

About Michael

Michael "Mike" Canet helps people create and grow wealth, protect and preserve it, and distribute it in the most tax-efficient manner. Whether an average American just entering into retirement, or a complex multi-generational family looking into protecting wealth, Michael helps clients maximize their assets and plan for the future using advanced tax planning. He uses retirement and estate-planning techniques to carefully allocate clients' assets so they can retire with added confidence, income, and tax-deferred wealth protection. He reminds his clients that it doesn't matter how much you make, rather it is how much you keep at the end of the day that really counts.

Michael is an active industry contributor to television, radio, and print. His numerous publications can be found in 100 different periodicals and journals across the country, including *WSJ, Forbes*, and *USA Today*. He has contributed to a variety of periodicals, journals and books, including *Successonomics* by Steve Forbes and the Amazon #1 Best Seller: *Surviving the Perfect Storm: How to Create a Financial Plan That Will Withstand Any Crisis*. He has been seen on every major network as a financial commentator, and has hosted a nationally syndicated television and radio show, "The Savvy Investor." You can find his talks and interviews on a variety of major network shows in Baltimore, including on FOX, NBC, CBS, and ABC.

Michael is quick to share his personal history, and how his upbringing influenced his approach to business and philanthropy. Mike grew up living in children's shelters and in the foster care system, experiencing various highs and dysfunctional lows. As he moved within the social welfare system, he recognized the many incredible people who provided him the stability and encouragement he needed to thrive. Today, Michael commits to giving back as much as he can by helping those less fortunate. These causes include the Maryland Volunteer Lawyer Service (where Michael was named Volunteer of the Year). Additionally, his position on the UB President Advisory Board helped them raise and donate over $150k to causes like Make-A-Wish, Ronald McDonald House, Ray's Summer Days, MD Food Bank, Generosity Global, Animal Welfare Society, Back to School Supply Programs, and a host of others.

Michael continues to put his family and loved ones front and center for himself, his firm, and his clients. He has been married for 39 years, and has two incredible sons. Michael takes great pride in the stability he has been able to provide to his own family, stating that he wanted to make sure they never experienced what he went through. A devoted family man and husband, he counts his blessings while at home, where he enjoys entertaining, cooking, and his avid wine collection. Michael splits his time between Ellicott City, MD and Melbourne, FL, and is an enthusiastic world traveler, exploring food and culture on five (and counting!) continents with his favorite travel partner, his wife.

More information:
- https://prostatisfinancial.com/

GLOSSARY
Investment Terms Definitions

The following terms and definitions are meant to be helpful in understating various investment and financial terms. The definitions provided are general in nature and are not intended to be a definitive explanation of the various financial terms contained herein. For a comprehensive and exhaustive explanation and understanding of the following terms, please consider using a dictionary or the internet for a more thorough and detailed explanation.

401(k) Plan:
Employer-sponsored, qualified plan that permits employees to make pretax contributions from their salaries to a profit-sharing plan, a target benefit plan, or a stock bonus plan. The great news is contributions and earnings grow tax deferred until withdrawn.

403(b) Plan:
A retirement plan for employees of non-profit organizations, public schools, and churches where employees can contribute a portion of their salary into a mutual fund or annuity. As with a 401(k) plan, the great news here is contributions and earnings grow tax deferred until withdrawn.

Adjusted gross income (AGI):
This is the income amount on which a person computes deductions that are based on, or limited by, a percentage of his or her income in order to figure out federal taxable income. AGI is determined by subtracting from gross income any deductible business expenses and other allowable adjustments (some traditional Individual Retirement Account annual contributions, SEP and Keogh annual contributions, and alimony payments).

Administrator:
A person appointed by a probate court to handle the estate of a person who died intestate (without a will). They have the same duties as an executor.

Advisor:
See definitions for Financial Advisor and Investment Advisor.

Annuity:
A contract that provides for a series of payments to be made or received at regular intervals. An annuity may be immediate, starting as soon as the premium has been paid, or deferred, starting at a designated later date. Annuities are commonly used to fund retirement. See fixed annuity or variable annuity.

Asset:
Property and tangible resources, such as cash and investments. Examples include stocks, bonds, real estate, bank accounts, and jewelry.

Asset allocation:
Investment strategy whose purpose is to enhance total return and/or reduce risk by diversifying assets among different types of stocks, bonds and money market investments.

Beneficiary:
An individual, institution, trustee, or estate that receives, or may become eligible to receive, benefits under a will, insurance policy, retirement plan, annuity, trust, or other contract.

Bond:
Basically an IOU or promissory note of a corporation, usually issued in multiples of $1,000. A bond is evidence of a debt on which the issuing company usually promises to pay the bondholders a specified amount of interest for a specified length of time, and to repay the loan on the expiration date. In every case, a bond represents debt-its holder is a creditor of the corporation and not a part owner, as is the shareholder.

Brokerage:
Security transaction executed through a "brokerage firm" or "broker/dealer" in stocks, bonds, mutual funds, options, or other investment securities. This term is often mistakenly used for the brokerage firm itself, but it referring to the transaction.

Certified Public Accountant (CPA):
An individual who has received state certification to practice accounting.

Commission:
The broker's basic fee for purchasing or selling securities or property as a registered representative.

Death benefit:
The payment made to a beneficiary from an annuity or life insurance policy when the policyholder dies. Also called face amount or face value.

Deductible:
Relating to health insurance, a predetermined amount the insured person pays for medical treatment before the health insurance coverage kicks in.

Defined benefit plan:
A company retirement plan, such as a defined benefit pension plan, in which a retired employee receives a specific benefit based on salary history and years of service, and in which the employer bears the investment risk. Contributions may be made by the employee, the employer, or both.

Defined contribution plan:
A company retirement plan, such as profit sharing, money purchase pension, 401(k) or 403(b), in which each participant has an individual account within the plan with benefits based solely upon amounts contributed and the past performance of that account. The participant bears the investment risk

Diversification:
Spreading investments among different companies in different fields. Another type of diversification is offered by the securities of many individual companies because of the wide range of their activities.

Dividend:
The payment designated by the board of directors to be distributed pro rata among the shares outstanding. Preferred shares generally pay a fixed dividend, while common shares pay a dividend that varies with the earnings of the company and the amount of cash on hand. Dividends may be omitted if business is poor or the directors withhold earnings to invest in plant and equipment. Sometimes a company will pay a dividend out of past earnings even if it is not currently operating at a profit.

Equity:
The ownership interest of common and preferred stockholders in a company. Also refers to excess of value of securities over the debit balance in a margin account. Also, the value of a property that remains after all liens and other charges against the property are paid. A property owner's equity generally consists of his or her monetary interest in property in excess of the mortgage indebtedness. In the case of a long-term mortgage, the owner's equity builds up quite gradually during the first several years because the bulk of each monthly payment is applied, not to the principal amount of the loan, but to the interest.

Exchange Traded Funds:
An investment vehicle traded on stock exchanges, much like stocks. An ETF holds assets such as stocks or bonds and trades at approximately the same price as the net asset value of its underlying assets over the course of the trading day. Most ETFs track an index, such as the S&P 500 or MSCI EAFE. ETFs may be attractive as investments because of their low costs, tax efficiency, and stock-like features.

Financial Advisor:
An advisor employed to provide advice on subjects related to investing and personal financial decisions.

Financial Plan:
A plan with stated goals and objectives pertaining to current and long-term investment needs of the individual.

Financial Planning:
Creating a plan with stated goals and objectives pertaining to the current and long-term investment needs of the individual.

FINRA:
FINRA is an independent regulatory organization empowered by the federal government to ensure that America's investors are protected. Also see NASD.

Health insurance:
Insurance that provides protection against financial losses resulting from illness, injury, and disability. In general, any insurance program covering medical expenses and/or income lost owing to illness or accidental injury.

Heir:
Individual who will receive assets upon the death of another.

Income taxes:
Taxes on income, both earned (salaries, wages, tips, commissions) and unearned (interest from savings accounts, dividends if you hold stock). Individuals and businesses are subject to income taxes.

Individual retirement account (IRA):
A tax-advantaged personal retirement account that allows a person to invest each year. Your contribution may be tax deductible depending on your adjusted gross income, whether you're married and whether your employer offers a retirement plan at work. A Rollover IRA accepts eligible employer-sponsored retirement plan assets.

Interest:
Amount charged by a lender to a borrower for the use of money. Interest rates are normally expressed on an annual basis.

Internal Revenue Service (IRS):
The federal agency responsible for administering and enforcing the Treasury Department's revenue laws, through the assessment and collection of taxes, determination of pension plan qualification, and related activities.

Investment:
A current commitment of money for a period of time, to obtain future payments or wealth to compensate the investor for the time the funds were committed, for the inflation that may affect them, and for the uncertainty of repayment.

Investment Advisor:
A person employed to render advice or analysis about securities/investments for compensation, registered with the SEC under the Adviser's Act of 1940 or their respective state. Does not include attorneys and accountants who give advice as a part of their professional practice.

Investment company:
A company owning a diversified portfolio of securities that are professionally chosen and managed on the basis of certain investment criteria. The most common type of investment company is the mutual fund.

Investor:
An individual whose principal concerns in the purchase of a security are regular dividend income and/or capital appreciation without unnecessary risk.

Liabilities:
A broadly defined term implying legal or financial responsibilities to others.

Life insurance:
Insurance coverage against death of a person to be paid to a

beneficiary when the insured dies. See term insurance, whole life insurance, universal life insurance, variable life insurance, or survivorship life insurance.

Liquid:
Description of the condition in which an individual has adequate cash and near-cash assets to meet current debt.

Long-term care:
Physical, mental, and social assistance provided to people who are unable to provide for themselves as a result of disability or a prolonged illness. Care ranges from providing personal care at home, such as bathing and dressing, to skilled nursing services in a nursing home.

Medicaid:
A program, funded by the federal and state governments, that pays medical costs for the poor. If your financial assets and monthly income are below certain allowed levels, Medicaid will pay nursing home and some home care costs if you are disabled.

Medicare:
A federal program that pays for certain health care expenses for people age 65 or older.

Morningstar:
A leading provider of mutual fund, stock, and variable-insurance investment information. An independent company, Morningstar does not own, operate, or hold any interest in mutual funds, stocks, or insurance products.

Mutual fund:
An open-end investment company that continuously offers new shares to the public in addition to redeeming shares on demand as required by law.

NASD:
Refers to the National Association of Securities Dealers, Inc. An association of brokers and dealers in the over-the-counter securities business. The association has the power to expel

members who have been declared guilty of unethical practices. The NASD is dedicated, among other objectives, "to adopt, administer, and enforce rules of fair practice and rules to prevent fraudulent and manipulative acts and practices and, in general, to promote just and equitable principles of trade for the protection of investors." The NASD has been replaced by FINRA.

Net worth:
The amount by which a person's total assets exceeds total liabilities.

Online:
A technology service provided over computers that are networked together. Usually refers to the Internet. Allows for interaction between people via computer.

Planning:
The act of contemplating objectives, desires, and variables to accomplish an objective. Example would be current investments, rates of returns and retirement income desired for an individual's financial plan.

Portfolio:
A group of securities held by an investor. They might include stocks, bonds, preferred stock, and cash.

Principal:
As it relates to power of attorney, a principal is the person who is no longer able to make decisions so the attorney-of-fact is granted the power to make those decisions.

Retirement Income:
The amount of income needed, on an annual basis, to live once the investor has retired. Can be pretax (the amount needed for spending plus the taxes due on that amount) or after tax (the amount needed for spending to meet their lifestyle excluding taxes).

Retirement Plan:
A person's unique plan for meeting his or her retirement obligations or an employer-sponsored tax advantaged program to accumulate assets for retirement of the plan's participants.

Return:
The dividends or interest paid by a company expressed as a percentage of the current price. A stock with a current market value of $20 a share that has paid $1 in dividends in the preceding 12 months is said to return 5 percent ($1/$20). The current return on a bond is figured the same way. Another term for yield.

Rider:
It's an amendment to an insurance policy that modifies the policy by expanding or restricting its benefits or excluding certain conditions from coverage.

Risk:
Uncertainty that an asset will earn its expected rate of return, and is generally measured using standard deviation.

Risk Tolerance:
Technically, it's the measure of an investor's ability to accept risk. Investors are often categorized as risk-indifferent, risk averse or risk-seeking.

Roth IRA:
A personal retirement savings vehicle created by the Tax Payer Relief Act of 1997 available for certain investors beginning in 1998. A Roth IRA allows certain investors to make non-deductible contributions annually, and provided certain requirements are met, offers (after owning the Roth IRA for 5 years) tax-free and penalty-free withdrawals for important specified financial needs as qualified distributions. Distributions after age 59½ are tax-free provided you have had the Roth IRA for five years before you withdraw funds.

Savings account:
A bank account established for the purpose of putting aside

money for future spending goals. Savings accounts normally earn a competitive rate of interest and are insured by the Federal Deposit Insurance Corporation.

Share:
Certificate representing one unit of ownership in a corporation, mutual fund, or limited partnership.

Social Security:
The government-sponsored program which is designed to provide basic pensions and disability income for U.S. citizens.

Standard deduction:
The amount a taxpayer who does not itemize his or her federal tax deductions can deduct in determining taxable income.

Stock:
Ownership shares of a corporation that provides the lender with a claim on a company's earnings and assets. Stock may be issued in different forms, including common and preferred. Holders of common stock are the last to be paid any profits from the company but are likely to profit most from the company's growth. Owners of preferred stock are paid a fixed dividend before owners of common stock, but the amount of the dividend doesn't usually grow if the company grows.

Tax deductible:
An item or expense subtracted from adjusted gross income to reduce the amount of income subject to tax. Examples include mortgage interest, state and local taxes, un-reimbursed business expenses, and charitable contributions.

Tax-deferral:
Paying taxes in the future for income earned in the current year, such as through an IRA, 401(k), SEP IRA or Keogh Plan.

Tax-deferred retirement plans:
A retirement plan in which you get to postpone current income taxes on pre-tax money invested or any earnings in an account

until you withdraw it from the plan. Such a plan may allow you to set aside part of your pay for retirement. Tax-deferred accounts include traditional and rollover IRAs and 401(k)s.

Trusts:
A legal arrangement in which an individual (the trustor) gives fiduciary control of property to a person or institution (the trustee) for the benefit of beneficiaries.

Vested:
The rights of an individual to receive benefits from employment, such as pension, sick leave, and vacation. Pension benefits are vested when the employee has worked a specified number of years. The person may then leave the employer for another job and still collect the accumulated amount at retirement.

Volatility:
The extent to which the value of an investment changes. Often used as a description of risk and measured as Standard Deviation.

 CPSIA information can be obtained
at www.ICGtesting.com
Printed in the USA
BVHW062007100920
588453BV00005B/44/J